ANGRY
ROBOT

Triumff

HER MAJESTY'S HERO

Being an OUTRAGEOUS & astounding alternate
history fantasy of ALCHEMY & SWORDPLAY from
the quill of that MASTER of action & adventure,

Mr. DAN ABNETT

"Triumff is a witch's brew of alternate history, hocus pocus,
cracking action and cheesy gags. Reads like Blackadder crossed with
Neal Stephenson. Don't miss it." — STEPHEN BAXTER

1988 Canadian Sailor Gives Up Olympic Dream To Save Others
1988 Eddie The Eagle Soars In Calgariy's Winter Olympics
1988 Smurph The Opposition Physio Saves Opponent
1988 French Telegram Moments Before An English Battle
1989 Mayo Man Shows Gentle Kindness In Rugby Moment

1992 Derek Redmond's Dad, Barcelona Olympic Games
1994 Canadian Fulfils His Dying Sister's Promise – Lillehammer
1994 Norwegian Gold Opens Eritrea Window To A New World
1995 Mandela Calms The Rage And Boosts The Strength
1996 Englishman Saves Frenchman And Loses His Dream
1997 Scouser Fowler Protests Opposition's Innocence
1998 There's Honour In The Battle USA V Iran World Cup
1998 Modern Aussie Refuses To Beat Noble Knight's Record
1999 French Philosopher Offers An English FA Cup Rematch

2001 Sailing Teams Refuse To Sail Until Opposition Ready
2001 Swede Refuses Umpire's Error To Give French Victory
2001 Italian Di Canio Stops An English Premiership Game
2001 Teenage Ghanaian, Sumaila Abdallah Gives Kiss Of Life
2001 American Armstrong Beats Cancer & Wins 7 Tours
2002 Millwall Stand Still And Watch Bournemouth Score
2003 Cycling's Gentlemen's Club Wait For Leader To Remount
2004 Accrington Stanley's Paul Cook Relives Eusebio's Honour
2004 Tackled & Bruised & Battered, Brazilian Runs On
2005 Australian Warne Applauds Englishman During Battle

2006 Unique Goalies' Union – Iranian & Mexican Brothers
2006 American Lehman's Prayer For Opponent's Wife
2006 America's Phil Mickleson Embraces Opposition
2006 Irish Golfer, Clarke, Declines Leprachauns' Help
2006 Irish Mcginley Saves American Rookie's Embarrassment
2006 Norwegian Helps Canadian & Loses Medal At Ski Sprint
2006 American Cheek Provokes A Charitable Chain Reaction
2006 Canadian Multi-Medal Winner Supports 'Right To Play'

2007 God Save Croke Park – Sport Prevails Over Auld Enemy

Acknowledgements

Particular thanks to Larry Cooney, Mick Daly, Jim Dierker and Paul Shillito and Cath Smith for all of their editorial help. Thanks also to the following friends who told me of their personal moments and observations of sportsmanship and kindness (some of which are still being researched for future editions):

Allen, Dave – Derek Redmond's Dad story
Barton, Patrick – 1908 Marathon story
Bassett, Ray – Fowler's Penalty story
Bland, Michael – Crisis managent
Bowe, Stephen – Management systems
Carpenter, David – Shamrock Rovers Heritage Trust
Conlan, Eamonn – Tom Kiernan story
Cooney, Larry – Sports editor
Cvekovitch, Peter – London Irish captain
Daly, Mick – Sports sage and adviser
Daly, Des – Irish rugby stats
Dawson, Jack – Inspirational Sportsman
Dawson, Geoff – Team mate
Deasy, Martin – Host and raconteur
Dierker, Jim the American Eagle – Rudi Story
Flannery, Vyvyan – Vendeé Globe race
Gibson, Mike – Paul McGinley story
Grimes, Gavin – McBoom online virals
Hall, David – cricket check
Hendry, Joe – Derek Dougan story
IRFU, Irish Rugby Football Union
Johnson, Alan – Palestinian Kidnapper's story
Kelly, Finbar – advisor
Lansdowne RFC
London Irish Amateur RFC
MacFarland, Paul – advisory panel, sports business
MacDonald, Davy – Web site design
McCarthy – Smith, David – Research
McMahon, Gerry – Paul McGrath story (next ed.)
Mullarkey Johnny – London Irish RFC
Mullarkey, Martin – LIRFC
Munster Fan – Martin Johnson story
Murphy, Billy – Joe Louis & Max Schmeling story

Murray, Willow – IRFU photo archivist
Murray, Eoin – Palestinian story
O'Connor, Eddie – Supernova
O'Shaunessy Bob – Limerick hurler's story
O'Shaunessy, Mick – Toulouse entertainment
Pitcher, Sharon – Leicester v Notts Forest story
Probyn, Jeff – Smurph the Physio 1988 story
Quirk, Brendan – rugby stories
Redman, Paddy – Captain Oates story
Revel, Maria – QPR & Italian football fan
Sheppard, Roy – helpful advice
Shillito, Paul – Editorial advisor
Smith, Adam – Softball story
Smith, Aran – an appreciator of fine sporting moments
Smith, Cian – French philosopher story
Smith, Clodagh – horse racing stories (next ed.)
Smith, Conor – St. Michael's Alumni past president
Smith, Lily – Trampolining, singing expert
Smith, Rory – Mexican and Iranian goalkeeper story
Smith, Sarah – Media analysis
Smith, Shane – First World War football story
Smith Davis, Alan – Vendeé Globe race story
Smith Davis, Leonie – Test marketing
Stevenson, Irene – Irish Times Library
Stores, Adrian – advisory panel marketing
Sweetman, Rex – Designer
Tozer, Joe – Marketing consultant
Tracey, Larry – Norwegian and Canadian skiers story
Webb, Geoff – Zatopek's package story
Zook, Ze – Photographic advisor

My thanks of course to the lovely Beverley,
whose patience knows no bounds.

Note on the term 'sportsmanship'
Sportsmanship may, to some, seem sexist. It is certainly not meant to be sexist. Sportsmanship applies to males and females equally. 'Sportspersonship' sounds too cumbersome.
'Man' is used as it is shorter and really refers to our species. This book includes amazing examples from truly great sports men and women.

Foreword
by Paul McGinley

As a participant or fan, great sport can transport us from the humdrum of daily life to a place where pretty much the outside world ceases to exist....sometimes.

It goes even further and touches our very soul to a point where the intense competitiveness stops and kindness in human nature shines through like a beacon before the intense competitiveness resumes again and we are left to ponder the significance of what we have just witnessed.

Intense competitiveness that also touches our soul is the essence of great sport.

This is a wonderful book. Read on.

Preface

Great Moments of Sportsmanship and Kindness

Some say professional sport has lost it soul.
Others say that all sport has lost its soul.
Not true.

Here is a collection of stories that people
haven't heard of,
or perhaps, have simply forgotten.

Stories that ordinary people can relate to......
Stories that happened in the heat of
the moment.....

True stories that
rekindle the real spirit of sport.....

Stories of great moments of
sportsmanship and
extraordinary sports people.

1908

A moving finish line, a wobbly Italian and a sympathetic Queen – Olympic Games Marathon

2.33 pm Friday 24 July 1908. The gun goes off in the grounds of Windsor Castle and the 1908 Olympic Games marathon starts. Italian Dorando Pietri, wearing his distinctive red shorts, is at the back of the pack of 54 marathon runners from 16 countries. He doesn't take the lead for another 24 miles. As Pietri runs through the increasingly crowded cobble-stoned streets around London, his brother, Ulpiano, rides behind him on a bicycle encouraging him and feeding him water and chianti.

After several hours of running Pietri enters the White City Stadium as outright leader. Only 27 athletes (representing 11 nations) finish the gruelling race. Pietri collapses several times and even runs the wrong way at one point. The packed stadium falls silent as Pietri stumbles. Officials surround Pietri. Queen Alexandra rises to her feet. Two officials (Irish doctors) take pity on Pietri, run over, take him by the arms and help him across the finishing line. He is consequently disqualified (for receiving help) and the second man across the line, American Johnny Hayes, is awarded the gold.

Pietri, however, had won the hearts of everyone who watched his agonising finish. As Pietri was

Dorando Pietri being helped over the line
Photograph PA Photos

not responsible for his own disqualification, the next day Queen Alexander decided to award him a gold cup.

The Times of London captured this magical moment: "A mighty roar went up from the whole assembly as he made his way to the tail end of the prize winners, and the shouts and cheers and applause and sympathy were renewed again and again when it came to his (Pietri) turn to climb up the broad red carpeted steps, placed almost where he had fallen for the last time at the end of his gallant struggle, and received from the hands of England's Queen the beautiful cup – her own personal gift."

Queen Alexander presents
a special cup to Italy's Dorando Pietri
Photograph PA Photos

Incidentally, the Marathon's odd distance (26 miles 385 yards) was introduced at the 1908 Olympic Games. The traditional distance – 26 miles – derived from the Athenian legend of Pheidippides, who had run to Athens to report the defeat of the Persian forces. He collpased and died shortly after. In 1908, King Edward VII and Queen Alexandria wanted the race to start at Windsor Castle outside the city and end in the new White City Stadium some 26 miles away and ending in front of the royal box which gave the race its unusual distance of 26 miles and 385 yards.

The 1908 games were surrounded by contro-versy. The Swedish team did not participate in the opening ceremony since their flag (and the

American flag) had not been displayed above the stadium. The American flag bearer refused to dip his flag to the royal box. The Finnish team marched with no flag rather than march under the Russian flag.

The British 400m runner, Wyndham Halswelle, won gold by running around the track on his own in a re-run. The original US winner of the 400 metre race was accused of interfering with the British runner (both countries' rules had different definitions of interference). The race was re-run – solo as three of the four original contestants were American and refused to participate.

The 1906 Mount Vesuvius volcanic eruption which devastated Naples meant that funds were diverted for the Olympic Games and a new venue was required. London was selected. From over 2,000 athletes (1971 men and 37 women) who competed, Pietri felt that he was the one who actually won and lost: "I am not the marathon winner. Instead, as the English say, I am the one who won and lost victory." Dorando Pietri in the Corriere della Sera of 30 July 1908.

"Instead, as the English say, I am the one who won and lost victory."

1912

Englishman Lawrence Oates selfless South Pole expedition

Captain Lawrence Oates is the 'very gallant gentleman' who left his tent and walked to his death in a blizzard, in the hope that he would save his expedition team mates by not allowing his own injuries to slow the team down any further. As he crawled out from the tent to face -40°C temperatures and a full blizzard, he achieved immortality with his famous British understatement and parting remark, "I am just going outside and may be some time."

Oates was a cool headed man with immense courage. Although his left leg was an inch shorter than his right leg (from a gunshot wound which shattered his thigh), he was an expert horseman and a respected military man. He however became disenchanted with army life after serving in the Boer War. He was so determined to leave the army that he paid £1,000 (approximately £50,000 today) to be allowed to leave and subsequently join Scott on his Antarctic expedition. Exploration was possibly in his genes as his uncle, Frank Oates was the naturalist and African explorer.

Oates was a member of Captain Scott's doomed Terra Nova expedition to the South Pole in 1912. They did not get on very well. Oates is reported to have made a diary entry "Scott's ignorance about marching with animals is colossal." He went on to say "Myself, I dislike Scott intensely and would chuck the whole thing if it were not that we are a British expedition."

Cecil Henry Meares & Lawrence "Titus" Oates
in the Stable during their expedition with
Captain Scott to the South Pole
Photograph PA Photos

Having raced to the Pole they realized that Norwegian Roald Amundsen and his team had beaten them to it. Scott and his team turned around and started the long trek back to their base camp. As the weather worsened, the team made very slow progress. Oates' frostbite made walking extremely difficult. He even slit his sleeping bag to fit his swollen feet in. He knew he was slowing the group down and therefore endangering everyone's lives. This is when he decided to disappear into the blizzard and gave up his life. His body was never found.

All the remaining comrades sadly died in what became Scott's disastrous South Pole expedition in 1912. Six months later their bodies were discovered by another expedition – just eleven miles from a large food depot.

Captain Lawrence Oates left the tent, for the last time, on his 32nd birthday, the 17th March 1912 (Saint Patrick's Day). It is most likely that he died that same day.

**"I am just going outside and may
be some time."**

1914

Warring German & British play football & celebrate Christmas

24 December 1914 was more than a moment of great sportsmanship and kindness. It was amidst the horrors and despair of humanity, in the stench-filled trenches of the First World War, when sportsmanship and humanity emerged as victors despite the tragic deaths of more than 8 million young men.

A stretch of trenches ran south from the infamous Ypres Salient for 27 miles to the La Bassée Canal. This was part of the infamous Western Front. In places the enemy were no more than 70, 50 or even 30 yards away. Enemies often shouted at each other, but as Christmas approached and gifts from the homelands reached the front line, the mood improved. A British Daily Telegraph correspondent reported that on 'one part of the line the Germans had managed to slip a chocolate cake into British trenches'.

A message was attached to it, requesting a ceasefire for later that evening so they could celebrate Christmas, as well as their Captain's birthday. They promised to put candles on the parapets of the trenches followed by a concert at 7.30 pm. The British accepted the invitation and sent some tobacco across to the Germans. At precisely 7.30 pm German heads appeared above the parapet and they started singing. Each song ended with applause from both sides.

Songs were sung again on Christmas Day. Rations were thrown to each other. After a while troops and officers climbed out of the trenches and walked into no man's land to meet each other. Mortal enemies became friends, exchanging gifts, tobacco, buttons, even free haircuts from a skilled ex-civilian German barbers. One German, a juggler, juggled in the middle of no man's land.

German and British troops mingle in no man's land
Photograph Imperial War Museum neg. no. Q50719

The diary of Kurt Zehmisch of the 134th Saxons recorded: 'The English brought a soccer ball from the trenches, and pretty soon a lively game ensued. How marvellously wonderful, yet how strange it was. The English officers felt the same way about it. Thus Christmas, the celebration of love, managed to bring mortal enemies together as friends for a time.'

There were several 'kick-abouts' recorded up and down the line.

And soon the magical moments were over. Captain J C Dunn, the Medical Officer in the Royal Welch Fusiliers, recorded: 'At 8.30 I fired three shots in the air and put up a flag with "Merry Christmas" on it, and I climbed on the parapet. He [the German] put up a sheet with "Thank you" on it, and the German Captain appeared on the parapet. We both bowed and saluted and got down into our respective trenches, and he fired two shots in the air, and the war was on again.'

**'The English brought a soccer ball
from the trenches, and pretty soon a lively
game ensued.'**

1915

Englishman refuses to play in FA Cup Final

Vivian Woodward was, arguably, England's greatest goal scorer. He joined Tottenham Hotspur football club in 1901 and later he moved to Chelsea in 1909. Between 1903 and 1911 he won 23 full caps for England and scored an incredible 29 goals, setting an English record that would last for nearly 40 years. Some say his goal scoring ratio of over a goal a game will never be beaten.

However some of the opponents may not have been the standard of today's teams. In one such game, French Amateur XI v England Amateur XI in 1906, at Parc des Princes, Woodward was reported to have missed a penalty on purpose as he believed the French full back, Fernand Canelle, had inadvertently handled the ball. This did not affect the result, with England going on to win 15-0. Woodward scored either four goals or eight goals (depending on whether you read FIFA reports or newspaper reports respectively).

He went on to captain Great Britain and Ireland's football team in both the 1908 and 1912 Olympic Games. The Great Britain and Ireland team won gold in both.

He joined the British Army in 1914 and fought in the First World War (and who knows, he

Vivian Woodward – England's greatest goal scorer?
Photograph PA Photos

may have been one of the British and German soldiers who played football together in no man's land on Christmas Day 1914) and was given special leave to play for Chelsea in the 1915 FA Cup final at Old Trafford as one-eyed, Bob Thomson was injured. However, Woodward refused to play when he heard that Thomson had recovered as Thomson had played in all the previous cup matches and Woodward had not. Chelsea lost. Woodward went back to the murky trenches of the Western front and was injured in 1916. Although he rose to the rank of captain, he never again played top class football.

"Woodward refused to play when he heard that Thomson had recovered as Thomson had played in all the previous cup matches"

1932

British fencer gives up Gold Medal as judges miss opponent's scores

In the middle of the 1930s Great Depression, unemployment soared and despair was rampant. The 1932 Los Angeles Olympic Games raised the spirits of both competitors and spectators.

Los Angeles, July 1932. A liner carrying participants (of the Games) is welcomed by the crowd
Photograph IOC/Olympic Museum Collections

Olympic fans crowd the train station
Photograph IOC/Olympic Museum Collections

A record crowd of 100,000 turned out to see the opening ceremony. World records were broken (18 were either broken or equalled). It was as if the Olympic Spirit transcended the depression and swept people into the euphoria of these very special games.

The games were condensed into 2 weeks for the first time (it was 79 days minimum prior to 1932). New technology was introduced including automatic timing and the photo finish for the track events. Another new idea was introduced – medal winners received their medals standing on a podium while the gold medallist's national flag was raised (as was the pride of each gold medal recipient).

One such athlete stood on the podium with great pride, having given up the ultimate moment in all athlete's lives - receiving a gold Olympic medal,

A packed stadium at the opening ceremony of the 1932
Olympics

on the winner's podium whilst her country's flag is hoisted. She was a 22 year old British fencer. Her name was Heather Seymour Guinness (known as Judy Guinness) and she was instead, going to receive a silver medal, despite being declared the winner of the final.

The judges declared her the winner having, in their opinion, beaten Austria's Ellen Preis in the final. However the judges had missed two touches scored against Guinness by the Austrian during the contest. Judy Guinness told the judges, knowing full well she would lose the gold medal which she had been told she had won. The gold medal was duly awarded to the Austrian.

(L to R) Heather Guinness (GBR), Ellen Preis (Aut), Bogen Erna (Hun). Having been declared the winner, Britain's Judy Guinness (left) takes the silver medal. Austria's Ellen Preis gets the gold medal
Photograph IOC/Olympic Museum Collections

Judy Guinness embodied the essence of the Olympic fair play spirit as an honest and honourable fencer. Only four sports have been contested in every Olympic Games since its conception in 1896. Fencing is one of those special sports and Judy Guinness was one of those special sportswomen.

'...the judges had missed two touches scored against Guinness by the Austrian during the contest ...Guinness told the judges...'

1936

Blond German helps a black American opponent during Hitler's Olympic Games

Jesse Owens sat despondently on the field watching his Olympic dream slip away. He had fouled his first two attempts at the long jump. He had just one more attempt left and he felt he was about to crash out of the 1936 Berlin Olympic Games. His German opponent, the 19 year old blond Carl Ludwig "Lutz" Long approached him and explained how he could avoid another foul by simply jumping from a point several inches behind the line. Owens had regularly jumped beyond the minimum 7.15 metres required to advance to the next round and he could afford to jump from a few inches short of the line.

Owens took the German's advice and sailed into the next round. In fact, Jesse Owens went on to win the gold medal for the long jump with a mighty leap of 9.06 metres. Although Long came second, he was first over to congratulate Owens. They were photographed together and they walked arm in arm to the dressing room.

Hitler wanted to use the 1936 games to show the world a 'resurgent Nazi Germany depicting Aryan racial superiority with inferior ethnic Africans'. James Cleveland "Jesse" Owens actually went on to win four gold medals at the Berlin 1936 Olympic Games: the 100 metres, the 200

(L to R) Naoto Tajima, Jesse Owens, Luz Long
Photograph PA Photos

metres, the 4 x 100 metre relay and the long jump (or 'broad jump' as it was known then). Hitler stormed out of the stadium.

Owens always maintained he owed his success of his overall athletic career to his junior-high track coach at Fairview Junior High, Charles Riley, who put him on the high school athletics team and even allowed Owens to train in the morning before school - as young Owens worked in a shoe repair shop in the afternoons.

Jesse Owens won four gold medals in Berlin 1936
Olympics Photograph PA Photos

Jesse Owens also knew how great a sporting gesture his young German opponent had made. Owens later said, "It took a lot of courage for him to befriend me in front of Hitler... You can melt down all the medals and cups I have and they wouldn't be a plating on the twenty-four carat friendship that I felt for Lutz Long at that moment."

Dr. Carl Ludwig "Lu(t)z" Long died in a British-controlled military hospital following the Allied Invasion of Sicily in July 1943. He was posthumously awarded the Pierre Coubertin medal for his Olympic actions and his true spirit of sportsmanship. Roads near the sports facilities in his home town of Leipzig and also in the 1972 Munich Olympia Park are named after him. Carl Ludwig "Lu(t)z" Long's medal, photos, and documents were donated to Leipzig's Sports Museum. The long jump victory is documented, along with many other 1936 events, in the Olympia Film (1938) by Leni Riefenstahl.

"It took a lot of courage for him to befriend me in front of Hitler... You can melt down all the medals and cups I have and they wouldn't be a plating on the twenty-four carat friendship that I felt for Lutz Long at that moment."

1948

A sad celebration, a standing ovation and Three Cheers from the opposition

Donald Bradman was, and arguably still is, the greatest cricketer of all time. The Australian was playing in what many expected to be his last innings in England. Such was the popularity of the great Australian that the whole crowd cheered him onto the pitch that day. The English cricket team even gave him three cheers when he reached the wicket at the Oval.

He was a true gentleman and one of the most unassuming sports stars the world has ever seen. He only needed to score four runs to keep his batting average, in test cricket, a stunning 100. Never before, or since, has this been achieved – a test cricketer with a test average of 100 runs.

Bradman was not aware that this was going to be his last test match. Neither was he aware that he only needed four runs to have a test match average of 100. It was however, as Bradman said, "a very emotional occasion because Yardley called all his fielders around him and they all gave me three cheers before I took the bowl." As Yardley swung his cap in the air each time for each cheer, so did all of the English team, and so too, did the whole crowd as they all showed their appreciation of the great Donald

Sir Donald Bradman, the world's best batsman
Photograph PA Photos

Perhaps it was also a farewell gesture, because it was probably Bradman's last test match in England and (possibly) his last test match ever. The crowd knew they were witnessing something special.

Unfortunately Bradman was then bowled out by Eric Hollies for a duck (nought). Many say that Bradman would have been affected by the unusual applause and the even more unusual, yet generous, three cheers from the English team and all of the fans. Bradman left the wicket and marched the long, lonely, walk to the dressing room. He did jog, up the steps despite the sadness in his heart. The world's greatest cricketer made a dignified exit.

Sir Donald Bradman died at home in February 2001 at the age of 92. Of the many accolades written about him one summed up this amazing sports star – "His greatest achievement was his humility and grace as a man."

"His greatest achievement was his humility and grace as a man."

For more on Sir Donald see 'Modern Australian refuses to knock noble Australian Knight's record 1998'.

1952

Last minute Czech Triple Gold runner reveals two finger touch technique

Emil Zatopek of Czechoslovakia, left, gives his all as he
heads to victory on the last lap of the Olympic 10,000
meter run at Helsinki, Finland, July 20, 1952. Alain
Mimoun of France follows Zaptopek
Photograph PA Photos

Having won gold medals in the 5km and 10km in
the 1952 Helsinki Olympic games (whilst breaking both Olympic records) Czech hero Emil
Zátopek felt pretty good and made an extraordinary, last minute, decision. He entered himself
into the marathon – never having competed in a
marathon before. He won it, took the gold medal
and, once again, beat the Olympic record.

Zátopek ran uniquely – with a rolling head, torso turning from side to side and face writhed in pain. His nickname, 'The Czech locomotive', came from his unusual wheezing and panting. All of his techniques were considered to be completely unorthodox and, in fact, an extremely inefficient style of running.

He pushed himself beyond the pain barrier. He once remarked: "It's at the borders of pain and suffering that the men are separated from the boys." When asked about how he appeared to be running whilst writhing in pain, he answered: "It isn't gymnastics or ice-skating, you know." He also maintained that he simply "was not talented enough to run and smile at the same time." In his 5km Olympic victory, he ran a 'ferocious' last lap in 57.5 seconds overtaking all three front runners. After winning, he once remarked, "But it was the finest exhaustion I've ever felt."

But beyond his unassuming, and often, colourful quotes lay a man who embraced the spirit of sportsmanship by being always willing to pass on advice to other athletes. One of his favourite tips was 'to always be relaxed'. He explained to others that gently touching the tip of your thumb with the tip of your middle finger always helped relaxation – even whilst running.

His training was intense. He used to run through the Prague woods wearing heavy army boots. He also used to run one hundered separate

400m sprints every day for a whole week.

He somehow managed a miraculous recovery in the next Olympic Games, Melbourne 1956. Having had a hernia operation a fortnight earlier, he finished sixth in the marathon. He used to say, "Essentially, we distinguish ourselves from the rest. If you want to win something, run the 100 metres. If you want to experience something, run a marathon." He retired in 1957.

Emil Zátopek was a Czech hero. He was also a member of the Communist Party and supported the Democratic Wing in the Czech Rising in 1968. He was removed from office and forced to work in a uranium mine. In 1970 Zátopek started work with the Czechoslovak Physical Training Association and was later associated with the Czech national sports institute. In 1999 he was voted the Czech Republic's greatest Olympic champion. He was also one of the kindest champions ever [see 1966 Czech Slips package to Australian at Airport].

He passed away at the age of 78 in 2000. He was awarded the Pierre de Coubertin medal (or the True Spirit of Sportsmanship medal) posthumously that same year.

"a man who embraced the spirit of sportsmanship by being always willing to pass on advice to other athletes."

1956

A kiss from his Russian opponent's mother for an Iranian wrestler

The Iranian people have a deep love of honour and nobility in sport. Athletes, like wrestlers, are expected to be 'pure, truthful and good tempered' first and foremost. After that they are expected to be 'strong in body'. Iranian (or Persian) wrestling is connected with Sufi Spiritualism and is an ancient, honourable tradition. In the elite training facilities known as Zurkhaneh, or "houses of strength", wrestlers participate in the ancient ritual where they learn to be 'pure, truthful and good tempered'.

One talented Iranian wrestler won the hearts of many with his outstanding sportsmanship. His name was Gholamreza Takhti. He eventually became the 1956 Olympic champion (he also won silver in both 1952 and 1960). In fact he won golds and silvers for over ten years at Olympic Games and World Championships between 1951 and 1962. He is a national hero as he epitomises honour, nobility and chivalry within the sports arena and even outside of it. To Iranian people, he symbolizes the essence of sport.

Takhti was deeply saddened by the terrible earthquake in western Iran (Boein Zahra) in 1961. He started walking the main streets of Tehran, asking people to donate money and to help the victims. Other sports champions followed his example and thousands of Iranians helped the victims.

Like many great sportsmen and women, Takhti, was alert to the sensitivity of others. After beating the world champion Anatoli Albul in Moscow, he noticed Albul's mother looking distraught. He went over to comfort her and is quoted as saying ""I'm sorry about the result, but your son is a great wrestler." Her face lit up and she kissed him right there and then.

On another occasion, he fought against the Russian Alexander Medved (gold medallist 1964, 1968 and 1972), who was carrying an injured right knee at the time. Takhti knew this and never once attacked the injured leg. He worked on the other leg instead – valuing honour more than victory. The Russian has since visited Takhti's grave many times in total respect for the great Iranian sportsman who died in 1968.

"Takhti knew this and never once attacked the injured leg. He worked on the other leg instead – valuing honour more than victory"

1958

Irishman saves lives and honour in Munich aircrash

Amidst the eery silence and instant shock, Harry Greggs lay on an ice cold runway surrounded by snow and the smashed debris of a lethal aircraft crash. The Munich Aircrash killed and maimed the world's most youthful and potentially, most exciting, professional football team, Manchester United's Busby Babes. 23 of the 43 people on the flight died.

Manchester United team group (L-R): Duncan Edwards, Eddie Colman, Mark Jones, Ken Morgans, Bobby Charlton, Dennis Viollet, Tommy Taylor, Billy Foulkes, Harry Gregg, Albert Scanlon, Roger Byrne
Photograph © PA Photos

More would have died had not one young player, Harry Greggs from Coleraine, raced back into the flames to save as many as he could, despite the aircraft captain Jim Thain's plea, "Run you stupid bastard, it's going to explode!"

When the propeller driven plane crashed on its third attempt to take off from the snow-swept runway, the fuselage split into two and young Greggs was hurled out of the plane and into the snow. While a burning fuel dump was about to explode, he stormed back into the flames to save his dying pals from the carnage. He rescued two players, Bobby Charlton and Dennis Viollet, and two strangers – a woman and her child (as well as her unborn baby). He dragged them out and across the snow.

The Busby Babes were young and talented. They represented hope and optimism in post war Britain. In fact many felt that if Manchester United could win the European Cup, England could also do well and maybe even win the World Cup that same year. There was great hope in the air.

The team captain and England international, Roger Byrne lay dead, along with Tommy Taylor, centre-back Mark Jones, midfielder Eddie Colman, forward Liam Whelan, winger David Pegg and defender Geoff Bent. The 21 year old, Duncan Edwards, deemed to be the finest foot-baller of his generation, lost his fight for life 15 days after the crash. Although he was given the last rites, the manager, Matt Busby, did survive and was released from a German hospital several months later.

The wreckage of the British European Airways plane
which crashed in Munich on February 6, 1958,
while bringing home members of the Manchester United
football team from a European Cup match
Photograph PA Photos

The aeroplane's captain, Jim Thain, was villified as the German authorities claimed that Captain Thain should have had the wings de-iced. Thain always maintained that the minimal ice was thawing and did not require de-icing. Years later, a British inquiry found that 'slush on the runway' was the 'sole cause of the crash'. Harry Greggs recently went out of his way to make a point of clearing Captain Tim Thain's name: "Private papers that were only released a few years ago show that the British government at the time did not want to embarrass the West German government so soon after the war ."

Sadly Captain Thain was dismissed by BEA. He never flew professionally again, and he died of a heart attack in the 1970s. However, Harry Gregg's bravery, kindness and honesty prevailed as he saved lives and later saved the honour of a dead man.

"Harry Gregg's bravery, kindness and honesty prevailed as he saved lives and later saved the honour of a dead man."

1960

Rudolph comes home to an integrated party

Of all the stories in this book, this is the most extraordinary because it's against all the odds, and oozes kindness combined with grit and talent. It eventually created a moment in 1960 that helped improve things for black people for many years to come.

This is the story of Wilma Glodean Rudolph. Born June 23, 1940 to Ed and Blanche Rudolph in Clarkesville, Tenessee, she was the 20th of their 22 children. Born prematurely, she weighed only 4.5 pounds and was sick right from the start. Unable to afford doctor's fees, her mother nursed her through measles, mumps, scarlet fever, chicken pox and even double pneumonia. She was later diagnosed with polio and told she would never walk. Blanche Rudolph never gave up on her little girl and discovered a treatment 50 miles away in Nashville. Twice a week they went there for two years until, with the aid of a metal leg brace, she was able to walk.

The whole family helped with the physical exercises at home. They all encouraged her. Finally, she would walk without crutches and braces and special shoes. They say it was then that she decided to become an athlete. Although she joined the basketball team, the coach didn't give her a game for three years. When she did get her

USA's Wilma Rudolph (R) holds on to take the
gold medal from Great Britain's Dorothy Hyman (L)
who takes the silver medal
Photograph PA Photos

game, she was soon spotted and invited to
Tennessee State for a summer sports camp.
A budding world champion was discovered.
At the tender age of 16, Rudolph ran in the 1956
Olympic Games representing the USA in their

women's 4 x 400 metres and won bronze. By 1960 and the Rome Olympic Games, she was ready to stun the world by becoming the first woman to win three gold medals in the 100m, 200m and 4 x 100m relay (as the anchor runner).

This extraordinary woman became the first female athlete to win several sporting awards (many of which were previously male only) including: The Sportswriters' Sportsman of the Year; European Sportswriters' Sportsman of the Year; James E. Sullivan Award for Good Sportsmanship; Christopher Columbus Award for Most Outstanding International Sports Personality; The Penn Relays; New York Athletic Club Track Meet; The Millrose Games.

Wilma had many amazing achievements but her greatest was to insist that her home-coming victory parade in 1960 had to be a fully integrated affair so that black and white could enjoy the parade. This was the first racially integrated event ever held in Clarkesville.

She continued to lobby and protest until segregation laws were later dismantled. In 1967 Vice-President Hubert Humphrey sought her advice in helping with outreach programmes for underprivileged kids in inner cities. Wilma set up the Wilma Rudolph Foundation, to continue the work of providing free coaching across a range of sports as well as academic support.

Wilma had more than grit, determination and an

explosive turn of speed. Against all the odds (of even walking), she was the fastest woman in the world. Most of all, she had kindness, generosity and grace.

Wilma wrote her autobiography called 'Wilma' in 1977 and it was later produced as a television movie. Wilma Glodean Rudolph died prematurely from cancer at the age of 54 on 12 November 1994. Three years later (1997) Governor Don Sundquist proclaimed 23 June (Wilma's birthday) as Wilma Rudolph Day in Tenessee. In 2004 the US Postal Service made a 23 cent stamp in her honour.

"Wilma insisted that her home-coming victory parade in 1960 had to be a fully integrated affair so that black and whites could enjoy the parade."

1960

America's Arnold Palmer helps the world to solve its problems

Arnold Palmer won 7 major golf titles as well as the hearts of a lot of sports fans. He won the Masters (1958, 1960, 1962, 1964), The (British) Open (1961, 1962) and the US Open (1960). He was also a member of the US Ryder Cup team (1961, 1963, 1965, 1967, 1971, 1973) and he captained the team in 1963 and also came back (when asked to be captain again) 12 years later in 1975.

When the British Open, known as 'the Open' was struggling to attract big overseas golf stars, Palmer turned up. Not only that, he encouraged others to do likewise. He was, to say the least, very influential in making 'The Open' the golf major it is today.

"When I first went to the British Open, in 1960, few Americans were in the habit of going over. People wanted to know why I made such an issue of it. I just always had the ambition of playing in the British Open, and winning it. I've got a strong feeling that golf is a great vehicle to bring nations closer together. If I could get all the war-torn nations of the world and have the warlords play golf together, I could solve the world's problems and we could all be peace-loving people. That may sound far-fetched, but it's what I believe."

Arnold Palmer points to his name on the press score-board showing his four under par total for 72 holes for the National Open tournament in Denver, Colorado, June 19, 1960. Palmer won the tournament with a score of 280
Photograph PA Photos

Arnold Palmer is one of golf's all time greats. He was nicknamed "The King," because of his golfing talent, his popularity and his trailblazing television profile (as TV emerged in the 1950s). In 1974 he was introduced into the World Golf Hall Of Fame. In 1998 he was awarded the PGA Tour Lifetime Achievement. His belief that sport can heal wounds and bring people together, despite intense rivalry and competition, is profound. Maybe his dream will one day be realised as nations compete in sport yet unite in the fellowship of sport.

"If I could get all the war-torn nations of the world and have the warlords play golf together, I could solve the world's problems and we could all be peace-loving people."

50

1964

Italian flying Red Head repairs Canadians & British sleighs

The Italians and the hometown Austrians were red hot joint favourites for gold medals in the four-man Bobsleigh event in the 1964 Olympic Winter Games in Innsbruck. The Canadians were considered to have an outside chance.

The Canadians stated their intent by breaking the Olympic record in the first heat and were leading the field by half a second. However they had damaged their axle and would soon be disqualified. So Italy's top bob sleigher, Eugenio Monti, and his mechanics turned the Canadian sled upside down and repaired the axle them-selves. The Canadians went on to win gold with the Italians taking Bronze. The Canadians were amazed.

It goes from great moments to even greater moments. Later in the two man bob sleigh event, the British team sheared a bolt. Seconds before Monti steered the Italian number one team down the breath-taking, hair-raising track, he shouted "Get an Englishman and a spanner to the finish and they can have my bolt."

Upon completion of their race, and despite enquiries from disbelieving Italian press, the bolt was duly taken from Monti's sleigh, rushed back up to the starting area and immediately attached

Eugenio Monti – An Honourable Italian
Photograph PA Photos

to the British Bob Sleigh. The British went on to win gold and, once again, the Italians took bronze.

The Italian press were furious with Monti and his team. However Eugenio Monti and his Italian team wanted to beat the best. To beat the best they knew they had to compete on equal terms. It was as if the sports press did not understand the true nature of sport, but the Italians did.

Monti, The Flying Red Head, was later awarded the "Pierre de Coubertin" award for fair play. He was an unusually talented sportsman. He was the best skier in Italy, winning national titles in slalom and giant slalom but had to retire in 1951 after tearing ligaments in both of his knees. The twenty three year old athlete didn't give up. He switched to bobsleigh and within three years won the Italian championship and by 1957 won the world championship. Eleven years later, at the age of 40, he won gold in both the two man and four man events in the 1968 Winter Olympic Games in Grenoble, France.

In Italy's Cesana Pariol (Turin Winter Olympic Games 2006), Turn 19 is named after Monti. After he died in 2003, they named the Cortina's bobsleigh track after The Flying Red Head, the great Eugenio Monti.

"To beat the best they had to compete on equal terms. It was as if the sports press did not understand the true nature of sport, but the Italians did."

1965

South African golfer gives his money away

South African born, Gary Player was a gifted golfer and philanthropist. After winning the 1965 US Open at Bellerive, St. Louis, Missouri, he donated his winnings to charity. He gave $20,000 to the USGA to start a junior golf foundation which today gives grants to grass-roots junior golf programs and programs for individuals with disabilities. He also donated $5,000 to a cancer charity. He wanted to give something back to his adopted home, America.

Player was against South Africa's apartheid system. He founded the Gary Player Foundation to promote and support education for South Africa's underpriviledged. He also supported the Blair Atholl School in Johannesburg which educates 500 students every year.

Player's famous black caddie, Alfred Dyer, fondly known as 'Rabbit', travelled with him around the world for 18 years. Rabbit paid his tribute to Player when he said "Because of Gary Player and caddying I was able to put my son through college at Princeton University. I tell all the young kids today to caddie. But a young black kid today don't want to caddie, he can make more money doing the wrong things, and that's a shame! Caddying was a great way to grow up, learn the game, stay out of trouble."

Gary Player
"The harder you practice, the luckier you get"
Photograph PA Photos

He became only the third golfer (after Ben Hogan and Gene Sarazen) to win all four major champi- onships (US PGA, US Open, US Masters and The 'British' Open). Player was the first non- American to win the Masters when he did so in 1961. He was the only 20th century golfer to win a British Open title in three different decades (1959, 1968 & 1974). He was a winning machine. His many tournament wins included: The British Open 1959, Masters 1961, PGA 1962, US Open 1965, British Open 1968, PGA 1972, Masters 1974, British Open 1974, Masters 1978.

Player was the first real international golfer as he travelled the world playing the game he loved. He continues to donate to worthy causes domestically and internationally.

"I've studied golf for almost 50 years now and know a hell of a lot about nothing." But he also said "The harder you practice, the luckier you get."

"After winning the 1965 US Open at Bellerive, St. Louis, Missouri, he donated his winnings to charity."

1966

Czech slips package to Australian at Prague Airport

Australia's Ron Clarke was an extraordinary athlete. He set 17 world records and beat the best in the world. At the peak of his career, in 1965, during a 45 day European tour, Clarke ran 18 races in 8 countries and set an astonishing 12 world records. Not only had he talent and technique, he had gritty determination. In the 1968 Olympic Games, in Mexico City's high altitude he fought and fought all the way in the 10,000 metres. But with such thin oxygen his body couldn't do what his mind told it to do. He staggered almost unconscious over the finishing line and collapsed, permanently damaging his heart. He finished 6th.

In fact, Clarke won almost everything except the most cherished (and excrutiatingly elusive) Olympic gold.

Clarke mostly coached himself. When asked why he failed to win an Olympic gold medal in Tokyo 1964, he suggested it was his poor choice of tactics and that a good coach would have helped him to win gold in the 10,000 and silver in the 5,000.

He was a wonderful runner and a great admirer of the great Czech Locomotive, Emil Zatopek (see 1952 Last Minute Czeck Triple Gold Runner

Ron Clarke was a wonderful runner and
Zatopek admired him greatly
Photograph PA Photos

Reveals Two Finger Touch Technique). Zatopek
once discreetly gave Clarke a package at Prague
Airport and told him not to open it until he was on
the plane. He also told him "Look after it. You
deserve it." It was Zatopek's 10,000 metres
Olympic gold medal from Helsinki 1952. Perhaps
the fearless Zatopek actually feared that Clarke
would not accept such a gift had he have opened
it before boarding the plane. Hence the instruc-
tions, laden with kindness. Respect and quiet
admiration from one great athlete to another.

**"Zatopek gave Clarke
a package at Prague Airport and told him
not to open it..."**

1968

Tanzanian's never give up – Akhwari the Marathon Man

After the marathon had finished an hour earlier and the medals ceremony was finished, people were slowly leaving their seats and emptying the Olympic Stadium in Mexico City, when an announcement came over the tannoy system. One last runner was about to make his way into the stadium.

Almost out of the cold darkness emerged a hobbling John Stephen Akhwari of Tanzania. With a bloody and bandaged leg, he completed the final lap as the remaining spectators cheered him on.

Although Akhwari had taken a bad fall much earlier in the race and knocked his head, got trampled on, cut his knee and some say, dislocated his joint, he picked himself up and started a long hobble home.

Having crossed the finish line, Akwari collapsed into the arms of the medical personnel who then took him to hospital. When asked, the next day, why he didn't stop when he was injured he famously answered "My country did not send me to Mexico City to start the race. They sent me to finish."

John Stephen Akhwari had travelled more than 11,000 km to race in the 1968 Mexico Olympic

Games. And the run the race he did.

Today Akhwari, amongst other things, continues to support the John Stephen Akhwari Athletic Foundation, an organization which supports Tanzanian athletes training for the Olympic Games.

His steely determination and grit is an inspiration to many athletes. His selfless work for Taninian athletes also inspires many others.

"My country did not send me
to Mexico City to start the race.
They sent me to finish."

1968

Portugal's Eusebio – the total gentleman

Manchester United had waited along time for their chance to become kings of Europe. They'd even lost half their potential European Cup winning team in the terrible Munich aircrash [see 1958 Irishman Saves Lives and Honour in Munich Aircrash]. And now ten years later they were in the final, trying to win their first (and England's first) European Cup. They were playing the great Benefica (who had the unstoppable goal scoring genius Eusebio).

Two years earlier, Eusebio was the top goal scorer in the 1966 World Cup Finals
Photograph PA Photos

It was the ultimate challenge for players like United's young talent George Best. Other players, like Bobby Charlton, who had survived the 1958 plane crash, were playing their hearts out for absent friends, team mates, town and country. The manager, Busby (who was given the last rites after the Munich crash), was there willing his team on. It was as if the world was willing Manchester United to win.

And then, in the closing stages of normal time, terror struck the hearts of Busby, Best, Charlton and the whole Manchester United side. Suddenly, out of nowhere appeared Eusebio with the ball, clean through on his own, inside the penalty box, about to score.

Eusebio breaks through and shoots in The European Cup Final at Wembley Stadium, on the ground is David Sadler
Photograph PA Photos

Eusebio shot from almost point blank range at the Manchester United goal – for what would have surely, won the European Cup.

Somehow Manchester's Alex Stepney saved the point blank shot. Eusebio stood there, amazed at first and then he started to applaud Stepney. Eusebio even tried to put his arm around Stepney to congratulate him as the intense game continued.

Stepney didn't know what was going on and encouraged Eusebio to rejoin the game immediately. Amidst the European Cup Final, Eusebio jogged away while still clapping his hands towards the opposition goalkeeper. United went on to win in extra time. Eusebio's talents and his ultimate sporting approach to the game won the hearts of football fans around the world forever.

"Amidst the European Cup Final, Eusebio jogged away while still clapping his hands towards the opposition goalkeeper."

1968

Welshman appeals on behalf of Nottingham opposition – Sir Garfield Sobers' World Record 6 sixes

West Indian hero and Nottingham captain, Gary Sobers was in great form as Nottingham played Glamorgan in Wales in the summer of '68. He made a world record by hitting six sixes in one over (from six consecutive balls).

Sobers opened by smashing bowler Malcolm Nash's first ball over the boundary. The second ball was dealt with similarly. By the time Sobers hit his third six from the third ball, the crowd sensed that history might be in the making. The fourth delivery from Nash was met with precision timing and hit for another six. The crowd held its collective breath as the fifth ball was delivered and Sobers went for it, hitting it high into the sky. Glamorgan fielder, Roger Davis, caught it and fell by the boundary. The umpires were unsure whether he was inside or over the boundary when he caught the ball. If he was inside, Sobers was out. The game stopped.

Umpires and players discussed the situation. Roger Davies apparently told the umpire that he fell across the boundary and therefore had not caught Sobers out. The 5th six was legitimate. The crowd anticipated history. Nash bowled the sixth and final ball of the over. Sobers went for it and drove the ball over the boundary, over the crowd and out of the ground altogether. BBC commentators said: 'He's done it. He's done it. My goodness it's gone way down to Swansea."

Sir Garfield Sobers in action
Photograph PA Photos

Sir Garfield Sobers was a magnificent batsman who, when asked how he was so successful – what was his batting technique – replied "When I see the cherry, I hit it." Sir Garfield Sobers was knighted in 1975 for services to sport. Roger Davis, his Welsh opponent, deserves an honour too for his honesty and total sportsmanship.

"Roger Davies apparently told the umpire that he, the fielder, had fallen across the boundary and therefore he had not caught Sobers out."

1969

America's Jack Nicklaus gives a 'Gimme' Ryder Cup

England's golfer Tony Jacklin had to make a two foot putt with the last shot of the match to draw the 1969 Ryder Cup (Britain and Ireland v the USA*). Although only two foot, it seems a long way when it is the culmination of several days of intense golf and you do not want to let your team mates down, let alone the local fans at Royal Birkdale and fans across Ireland and Britain watching on TV.

Even top professionals miss short putts when under huge pressure. His opposite number, the great Jack Nicklaus, bent down, picked up Jacklin's ball marker and declared it a 'gimme' (where the player doesn't have to attempt to putt the ball as the opposition generously assume the player would have putted the ball into the hole). Nicklaus famously conceded the putt, saying afterwards, with his arm around Tony Jacklin's shoulder, "I know you would not have missed that."

This magical moment is considered by many to be one of the greatest moments of sportsman-ship. Nicklaus said later: "I'm amazed at the attention that got because at the time I didn't think it was a big deal, I simply thought it was the right thing to do. It didn't make any difference to the result because we were going to retain the

The 1969 battle between American Jack Nicklaus (L)
and Britain's Tony Jacklin (R)
Photograph PA Photos

Cup either way, so I didn't want to take the
chance that he might miss the putt and have his
stature diminished. Tony was a hero and, as the
Open champion, was so important to the game in
Britain."

Jacklin was a gentleman, a sportsman and
demonstrated the respect and sportsmanship
that golf engenders.

**"Nicklaus bent down, picked up Jacklin's
ball marker and said 'I know you would not
have missed that'."**

** Note: Today the Ryder Cup is played between Europe
and the USA.*

Pele & Bobby Moore embrace each other after their
classic World Cup encounter in 1970
Photograph Action Images

1970

England's Sir Bobby Moore surrenders World Cup with valiant honour

England were the world champions. Brazil were the champions in waiting. Many felt that this 'clash of the champions' should have been the 1970 World Cup Final itself. The flowing match lived up to all expectations. It was a breathtaking game. The stunning brilliance of the Brazilians. The cool calm of the ultra talented English side. Up high in the altitude and in the searing afternoon heat (98 degrees) in the wonderful Estadio Jalisco in Guadalajara.

England had previously won in 1966 world cup in the most memorable World Cup Final of all time, beating West Germany 4-2 in extra time in Wembley with a hat trick from Geoff Hurst, one goal of which is still disputed to this day. And now England travelled to Mexico as holders. The 1970 team was even better. So too were the Brazilians.

The 1970 group stage match was an intense game of football played in the bright burning heat. Brazil eventually won by the narrowest of margins, 1-0 from a goal from the young Brazilian striker Jairzinho. He became renowned for both scoring in every game in the 1970 World Cup Finals and for his unique celebration: after every goal he scored, he always fell to the ground, blessed himself and prayed briefly.

All afternoon, England's magnificent World Cup winning captain, Bobby Moore, battled against the world's greatest footballer, Brazil's Pele. At the final whistle, Moore and Pele sought each other out and swapped their sweat soaked shirts of honour. They stopped for a moment, embraced, shook hands and spoke to each other with great warmth.

Years later, when Bobby Moore had tragically died from cancer (in 1991 aged 51), Pele is reported to have said, "He was my friend as well as the greatest defender I ever played against. The world has lost one of its greatest football players and an honourable gentleman."

To this day, you can still see the total respect and warmth these fierce rivals had for each other. The photograph on the previous page tells the tale. Warmth, respect and honour in opponents.

"At the final whistle, Moore and Pele sought each other out and swapped their sweat soaked shirts of honour."

1973

England's rugby captain, John Pullin – 'at least we turned up'

In 1973 the English rugby team travelled to Dublin whilst Wales and Scotland had the previous year refused to fulfil their fixtures in Dublin's Lansdowne Road because of the 'troubles' in Northern Ireland. The respective authorities said they could not guarantee the safety of their players and supporters.

When the English team ran onto the oldest international rugby ground in the world, Lansdowne Road, the English team were greeted with an 8 minute standing ovation from the Lansdowne crowd.

One of England's stars, the fleet-footed David Duckham, did express concern to his Lions' team mate and Irish stalwart Willy John MacBride. He immediately invited the newly-wed England winger to bring his wife over for the weekend, as Macbride's wife would host the young Mrs. Duckham personally. Duckham and the English team duly came.

The plan was for both teams to walk out together as a sign of unity, but such was the extraordinarily enthusiastic reception from Lansdowne Road's 50,000 spectators that England were ushered out first to take their due applause. Some say it lasted eight minutes, others say five minutes. Either way it was a long time for a standing ovation – but that's what the English team received that day.

England Rugby Team that visited Ireland in 1973
Back row.(L to R) CB Stevens, PJ Warfield, FE Cotton, RM Uttley, AG Ripley, CW Ralston, PJ Dixon & AM Jordan. Front Row. A Neary, PS Preece, SJ Smith, JV Pullin (Capt), DJ Duckham, AJ Morley & AR Cowman.
Photograph Willow Murray

At the post match dinner speech, England's Rugby Captain, John Pullin stood up and famously said "We might not be very good, but at least we turn up" (England were beaten 18-9). The assembled crowd stood up and gave another standing ovation.

To quote the official history of the Irish Rugby Football Union: "For over a century the happenings on the field of international rugby have stirred men's emotions but it is doubtful if there was ever a more emotional scene than that at Lansdowne Road when the English side ran on the field. The entire concourse to a man stood and applauded the English team for a full five minutes. It was hardly material that Ireland won a close match, 18-9, in which England missed more chances than they took."

In fact during the more recent controversy about whether England should play in Ireland's Croke Park, Irish President, Mary Robinson, suggested that England should receive the same 1973 Landsdowne Road welcome when they arrive in Croke Park in 2007 (see 2007).

To this day, John Pullin is hailed as a true sporting hero in Ireland. When he turned up, 34 years later, at a dinner in Dublin the night before the famous Ireland v England game at Croke Park, he received a special award from the Ireland Funds (charity), and he, once again, received a standing ovation for several minutes from an Irish crowd who truly love this English captain.

**"We might not be very good,
but at least we turn up."**

1973

Englishman, Mike Hailwood, rescues Italian from F1 inferno

Mike Hailwood has been described as an icon of motor bike racing "just as James Dean and Marilyn Monroe are icons of pop culture," and one hell of a guy. A revered legend he won world championships at 500cc in 1962, 1963, 1964 &1965; 350cc in 1966 & 1967 and 250cc in 1961, 1966 & 1967. Then in 1978, after a self imposed eleven year retirement from bikes, he made a 'fairytale comeback' to win another Isle of Man T.T. and with it, his 10th World Championship.

The multi talented Mike Hailwood
Photograph PA Photos

During his retirement from motor bike racing, he took up F1 car racing. In one such race, the 1973 South African Grand Prix at Kyalami he rescued his competitor, Clay Regazzoni, who lay unconscious and trapped in a burning wreck. One of the side-mounted fuel tanks on Regazzoni's car exploded on impact after a crash and immediately burst into flames. In a typical act of bravery, Hailwood leapt out of his car and with total disregard for his own safety, rushed into the flames. Standing amidst burning fuel tanks he managed to unlock the seat belt whilst catching fire himself. He extinguished his own flames and went back to "Regga" and with the help of a marshall pulled him from the burning wreckage. Regga survived.

Hailwood was later awarded The George Medal, Britain's highest honour for civilian bravery, for his heroic rescue of his competitor and fellow sportsman.

"In a typical act of bravery, Hailwood lept out of his car and with total disregard for his own safety, rushed into the flames."

1973

Northern Ireland's striker & visonary peace maker – Derek Dougan

Derek Dougan was a professional footballer, a prolific goal scorer and he represented Northern Ireland at the highest level (including World Cup) for fifteen years. He was a controversial chairman of the Professional Football Players Association (who improved players' rights) and who also had a vision of peace and unity in a land torn apart by violence and hatred.

Derek Dougan, Wolverhampton Wanderers, Northern Ireland and United Ireland
Photograph PA Photos

Derek Dougan had a vision of a united Ireland battling together against the best in the world. In fact, he believed, like George Best, that a united Ireland football team could take on the best in the world.

And he made it happen. In July 1973, during the height of the troubles in Northern Ireland history was made. The north and south of Ireland united to play the champions of the world, Brazil with their star studded team including Jairzinho, Rivelino and Paulo Cesar.

Dougan, Northern Ireland's captain and Johnny Giles, the Republic of Ireland's captain, managed to persuade their respective best players to play. The united team was officially called the Shamrock Rovers XI.

(Back L-R) Miah Dennehy, Tommy Craig, Paddy Mulligan, Martin O'Neill, Derek Dougan, Allan Hunter, Liam O'Kane. (Front L-R) Bryan Hamilton, Pat Jennings, Tommy Carroll, John Giles, Don Givens, Terry Conroy, Mick Martin

Photograph Irish Times Library

Played in the world's oldest international rugby ground, Lansdowne Road (where incidentally, the North and South do play as a united rugby team), it is still, today, deemed to be one of the most historic events in Irish sport. The first and only time the North and South of Ireland played together in a football match.

At a 35 year anniversary dinner, Northern Ireland player and now Aston Villa manager, Martin O'Neill said "Great credit must go to Derek Dougan." O'Neill went on to say, "For him to have that great foresight with the political backdrop of that time was really fantastic, where people were telling him he had to be careful. He should take great credit for what he did. It really was an incredible event."

It was a thrilling game of football with Brazil winning 4-3 and Derek Dougan scoring for Ireland.

Non-stop action from Ireland v Brazil 1973
Photograph Irish Times Library

End to end action from the Ireland v Brazil 1973
Photograph Irish Times Library

Derek Dougan never played for Northern Ireland again. Although he was 35 years old then, some say that he knew he would never be picked again after this game.

Coincidentally, Northen Ireland's finest footballer (and some say the world's best), George Best, many years later, called from his death bed for a United Ireland football team. He believed a united Irish side could be a force if they pooled their resources. "At any given time, both the Republic and Northern Ireland have had some great world-class players. I just believe in trying something. If it doesn't work, at least you've tried. I just hope it happens in my lifetime." Sadly, George died soon afterwards but his coffin was lovingly carried by his Northern Ireland captain, friend and visionary, the late, great, peace-making, Derek Dougan.

"History was made. The North and South of Ireland united to play the best in the world."

1973

Multi-tasking Irish International rugby player and referee

Scotland were playing Ireland in Murrayfield, Edinburgh on a foggy Saturday in February 1973. In the heat of this closely contested match, Andy Irvine, the Scottish fullback stepped up and dropped a goal from 'a distance'. It was such a distance that neither the crowd nor the referee could see whether the ball had made it over the cross bar for 3 points.

Tom Kiernan, Ireland and the British & Irish Lions
Photograph PA Photos

The only person in the stadium, and more importantly on the field, who could actually see whether it was a successful drop goal was the

80

Irish captain, Tom Kiernan as he was the nearest to the posts. The 34 year old 54 cap Irish hero and ex Lions captain immediately raised his arm to signal the goal for the opposition.

Scotland took the lead and went on to win 14-9.

Although this turned out to be Tom Kiernan's last game for Ireland, he was capped by Ireland over 14 seasons and was the first player to score 100 points for Ireland (February 1969). A year earlier he had broken George Stephenson's points record (89 points) for Ireland, a record that had stood for 38 years.

Tom Kiernan is a sports hero in Ireland and over-seas. He is also an honest man.

"The 34 year old 54 cap Irish hero and ex Lions captain immediately raised his arm to signal the goal for the opposition."

1974

South African Johannes Van Heeren respects receiving a good punch – the 1974 Lions '99' call

The British and Irish Lions comprise the best rugby players from Ireland, England, Scotland and Wales. Every four years they go on tour.

During the 1974 Lions rugby tour of South Africa, the squad developed the infamous '99 call' in response to the violent nature of many of the games in South Africa as a means of protecting team members by a total unified response from all the Lions players - to begin fighting.

When the Lions captain, Irishman, Willie John MacBride, called '99' in the Boet Erasmus Stadium, all the Lions players on the pitch threw punches. The full back, Welshman JPR Williams, was some 50 yards down the pitch on his own. So he had to run half the length of the pitch to find someone to punch. By time he arrived, the only man not being punched was the massive second row Johannes Van Heerden. JPR duly launched himself at Van Heerden, the biggest man on the pitch. JPR was several inches smaller and at least a stone lighter.

JPR hit Van Heerden and knocked him out. At the after match dinner the players mingled. Van Heerden sought out JPR Williams and asked him if JPR was the guy who punched him? When

JPR admitted that indeed he was, Van Heerden told him that 'it was quite the finest punch I have ever received.' Honour amongst men.

The victorious 1974 Lions
Photograph Getty Images

"It was 'the finest punch I have ever received.' "

Note: Today throwing a punch is a red card offence. In the 1970s it was not.

1975

A small guy never gives up and makes the big time

Daniel Rudy Ruettiger had a dream. He wanted to play American Football for America's most famous football university, Notre Dame, otherwise known as the 'Fighting Irish'. He didn't have it easy. He was one of fourteen children. He scored average grades and seemed to have average athletic ability. After high school, he joined the Navy and later worked at a power plant. His best friend died at the plant and this triggered Rudy to pursue his dream. He joined Holy Cross Junior College at the age of 23 and applied to transfer to Notre Dame University three times. Ruettiger was rejected three times. After discovering he was dyslexic, he passed his tests and was finally accepted (on his fourth attempt) into his beloved Notre Dame. He was tiny for a collegiate player (5'7" and 165 pounds).

Through his determination, he won a place on the scout team that helped Notre Dame's first team practise. He was still desperate to play for his beloved Notre Dame. In 1975 during Rudy's final year, and in Rudy's last chance to play for Notre Dame at home, the head coach, Dan Devine, put him in the squad.

And then Rudy came on and participated in two plays. In the second and final play, he made a tackle ('sack') on the opposition, Georgia Tech quarter back (which is all his Notre Dame stat line has ever shown). However Daniel Rudy Ruettiger is the only recorded Notre Dame player ever to be carried triumphantly off the field on his team mates' shoulders.

Rudy Ruettiger got to play for Notre Dame
Photograph PA Photos

They made a film about this extraordinary 'ordinary' guy in 1993 and called it, 'Rudy'*. He once again was a celebrity and was invited to the White House, to watch his movie with President Clinton, Joe Montana and Colin Powell. Rudy was quoted as saying "That's pretty exciting. All I did was make a tackle. Think about it, you know? I didn't win any super bowls, I didn't become the president, I didn't win any wars... I never quit."

"I never quit."

* NB In the movie, Head Coach Dan Devine is portrayed as 'the heavy' coach who refused to let Rudy dress up in the kit, let alone play. Devine did pick Rudy and intended playing him.

1976

Shun Fujimoto shattered knee doesn't affect the team

Shun Fujimoto was brought up in a Japanese tradition of self sacrifice. He was part of a Japanese gymnastics dynasty that had previously won four consecutive Olympic titles between 1960-1972. By the time Shun Fujimoto got to Montreal in 1976 they felt almost obligated to continue winning. In fact Shun said 'We never thought of losing in Montreal. We wanted to preserve Japanese gymnastics history which was kept for a long time. So it wasn't pressure. But it was our way to keep our past alive.'

The outstanding Soviet team had other plans and they took the lead by just more than one point.

It was now Shun's turn to complete the pommel horse routine with precision, balance and fitness. Few knew the excruciating pain he endured with each movement as he had broken his kneecap during an earlier floor routine with his final tumbling run. During and after the horse routine, he couldn't show pain to the judges as he "did not want the judges to think that I was hurt."

Next came the rings. As he was lifted up 8 foot off the ground towards the rings, he thought "I had to do it for me. And for the team. I was really good at the rings so I was confident of

Shun Fujimoto in pain & in plaster but with his 1976
Gold Gymnastics medal
Photograph PA Photos

doing it." His routine was almost perfect. Although he had yet to complete a highflying dismount from a height of 8 foot. He finished with a twisting triple somersault landing and dislocating the already broken kneecap as well tearing ligaments. The pain sliced through him 'like a knife'. But he somehow landed on his feet held his arms out, kept his balance and smiled at the crowd. He achieved his best ring score of his life. "I did not think of failing on the rings. The pain was unexplainable. I wasn't thinking what have I done? I couldn't think that much."

He could not now continue and had to withdraw with three rounds to go. However his team was so inspired by him that they went on to win by 4/10ths of a point 576.85 v 576.45. Shun refused aid and hobbled up to receive his gold medal with his team mates. "I was so relieved that I started crying because I had responsibility for all of us. We cried together. It was so difficult during the ceremony. But my team mates helped take me there."

"The pain sliced through him 'like a knife'. But he somehow landed on his feet, held his arms out, kept his balance and smiled at the crowd."

1981

German pallbearer lays his old American adversary to rest

Fighter Joe Louis, nicknamed the Brown Bomber, poses
in his boxing apparel in Pompton Lakes, N.J.. Louis
achieved the world heavyweight title in June 1937 and
held it until May 1949
Photograph PA Photos

Joe Louis is an all time great boxer. 25 consecutive title defences and 12 years as a world champion. Only one loss in his first 62 fights (a total of 65 wins out of 68 fights). But his greatness went far beyond the stats books as he lifted America when it was down (during the Great Depression of the 1930s). He even united blacks and whites in an unprecedented way when he beat the German Max Schmeling in 1938 and created harmonious joy across America.

Louis's sportsmanship and soft-spoken dignity contributed towards his status of an American idol.

Two years earlier, in 1936, Schmeling surprised everyone when he traveled by boat to New York and beat the highly rated (but not then world champion) Joe Louis (who suffered his first loss). Schmeling had been world champion from 1930-32.

By time the rematch came around Nazi Germany was flexing its muscles and America was still suffering form the depression. President Roosevelt reputedly invited Louis to the White House to issue words of encouragement. Previously Gobbels (Hitler's propaganda Chief) had used some of the first fight's footage in a propaganda film. Two thirds of radio-owning Americans tuned in to hear the broadcast. It was over in 124 seconds with Louis winning savagely. The country exploded into its first racially integrated party. "There was never a Harlem like the

Harlem of last night," reported the New York Daily News. "If you take a dozen Christmases, a score of New Year's Eves, a bushel of July Fourths and maybe, just maybe, you'd get a faint glimpse of the idea."

Max Schmeling, World Heavyweight Boxing Champion (1932) many years later, carried his old adversary's coffin
Photograph PA Photos

The New York World-Telegram reported: "One hundred years from now some historian may theorize, in a footnote at least, that the decline of Nazi prestige began with a left hook delivered by a former unskilled automotive worker who had never studied the policies of Neville Chamberlain and had no opinion whatever in regard to the situation in Czechoslovakia . . . ."

Max Schmeling returned home to Germany alone. He went on to save several Jews from Nazi gangs. He was eventually recruited into the army, survived the war and finally started a Coca Cola bottling franchise. Meanwhile, after his boxing career ended, Joe Louis fell on hard times. It was reported by many that Schmeling not only sent financial assistance to Louis from time to time, but that he paid for Joe Louis's funeral when the great man, 'the Brown Bomber' was buried in 1981. It is a fact that he did carry his old adversary's coffin.

Louis was pictured on a 29 cent commemorative postage stamp issued by the Postal Service in 1993. Max Schmeling died in 2005 at the age of 99. Neither will ever be forgotten.

"He carried his old adversary's coffin"

1981

Competing American and Norwegian hold hands in Marathon

Dick Beardsley (USA) leads Inge Simonsen (Norway)
in the final stages of the London Marathon, with the
Houses of Parliament in the background.
The two runners both won the Marathon, with a time of
2 hours, 11 minutes, and 48 seconds
Photograph PA Photos

As they pounded the streets from Greenwich Park, in south east London, to Buckingham Palace, American Dick Beardsley, and Norwegian Inge Simonsen attempted to break each other at various stages of London's first ever public Marathon. The 24 year old American and the 25 year old Norwegian repeatedly tried to find a way to break each other during this, the most arduous of races.

After 26 miles and 2 hours, 11 minutes and 48 seconds of gruelling competition, Beardsley and Simonsen decided they simply couldn't break each other and agreed to share the win by crossing the finishing line holding hands and effectively declaring a most honourable draw.

The Norwegian and the American, ahead of the other 6,253 runners, crossed the line holding hands in a deliberate dead heat.

"After 26 miles & 2 hours, 11 minutes & 48 seconds of grueling competition...they decided to call it a draw & hold hands crossing the line."

1988

Canadian sailor gives up Olympic dream to save 2 Signapore sailors

24 September 1988 and the seas around Pusan (near Seoul) suddenly turn dangerous. 15 knot winds turn into to 35 knot winds. Two Signapore sailors get into serious trouble. Four metre waves rise up around them.

Canadian Lawrence Lemieux was sailing in a separate race and looking like a strong medal contender as he was in second place in the fifth of seven races in the Finn class. An Olympic medal seemed within his grasp – the main question was which colour. Then Lemieux spotted the other two sailors in danger, in a separate race (the two man 470 class). Both had fallen out of their boat. Joseph Chan was being dragged further out to sea and the other one, Shaw Her Siew, was hanging on for life by clutching the capsized boat.

Lemieux immediately left his race and went after Joseph Chan who was drifting away from his boat. In increasingly difficult conditions, Lemieux sailed against the wind and into the four metre waves to get to Chan and successfully dragged him aboard. Lemieux's boat was now taking on water. Lemieux then rescued Shaw Her Siew.

Had he not have gone after them immediately, at least one may have died as the waves were so high "you couldn't see the big, orange course markers when you were between troughs. So looking for someone's head would have been like looking for a needle in a haystack," said Lemieux.

Having secured both sailors' lives, he waited for a rescue boat, transferred the grateful sailors and went back to his race. The moment was gone. His Olympic medal hopes evaporated. He finished 22nd out of 32 boats.

The International Yacht Racing Union jury decided that Lemieux should be awarded second place. None of his opponents challenged the decision. He did not win a silver Olympic medal at the awards ceremony but he was awarded the Pierre de Coubertin Medal for Sportsmanship. Lawrence Lemieux was also later inducted into the Alberta Sports Hall of Fame

"Having secured both sailors' lives...the moment was gone....his Olympic medal hopes evaporated."

1988

Eddie the English Eagle soars in Calgari's Winter Olympic Games

Into the crisp cold air, Eddie Edwards soared. Olympic crowds cheered as the English plasterer, risking life and limb, flew in the 1988 Winter Olympic Games in Calgary, Canada. Although he came 56th out of 57 competitors (the 57th was disqualified), he won over the Olympic audience over with his true Olympian spirit of competing regardless of the size of the challenge. Ski jumping in England does not get a lot of support. He was totally self funded.

Britain's First Olympic Ski-Jumper. Eddie "The Eagle" Edwards
Photograph PA Photos

He was handicapped by his weight – he was almost 1.5 stone (9kg) heavier that the next heaviest competitor. He was also short sighted and had to wear heavy thick lenses in his glasses which regularly fogged up as he soared up to 90 metres through the cold air.

When asked if he was afraid of jumping, he replied "Of course I was. There was always a chance that my next jump would be my last. A big chance." True sports lovers admired his honesty, enthusiasm and courage. His warm and affable personality won him many friends.

For the first time in the long and winding history of the Olympic Games, an individual athlete was mentioned in the closing speech. The president of the Olympic Games highlighted Eddie The Eagle for his sporting contribution: "At this Games some competitors have won gold, some have broken records and one has even flown like an eagle." At that magical moment of sporting appreciation, 100,000 people in the stadium cheered and roared 'Eddie! Eddie!' a sportsman who took on the highest challenge against all the odds.

**"There was always a chance that my next jump would be my last.
A big chance."**

1988

Smurph the opposition physio, saves rugby player's knee

Jeff Probyn was strong as an ox. As a rugby prop forward at representative level – you have to be. You also have to have excellent scrummaging technique, stamina and overall ability to play rugby. He had all this and more. In fact he was an up and coming star and was soon to be selected by England to represent his country.

A few weeks prior to his selection to play for England, Probyn was representing London, whilst playing against The North (of England) in what was then the Division Championship, in Wasps ground in Sudbury, London. In a horrible moment he was hit hard as he held the ball and his knee gave. He knew instantly it was bad. As he collapsed, thoughts went through his mind that perhaps...this game was over for him and perhaps his chance to play for England was over too. He feared the worst, as if the ligament was torn completely it was a serious operation.

He had, in fact, slightly torn the medial ligament which could mean 6-8 weeks out of the game effectively missing the start of the Six Nations Championship. Realising it was a potentially serious injury, the opposition physio, Kevin 'Smurph' Murphy ran onto the pitch and immediately tended the injured player. Smurph is a top physio (and had been the England Physio for many years). Smurph stabilised the knee and spent the rest of the day 'putting me right'. His expert handling of Probyn's damaged knee accelerated Probyn's recovery to just two weeks.

Jeff Probyn, one of England's finest prop forwards might never have played for his country but for the opposition physio's help
Photograph PA Photos

He had never met Kevin Murphy before, but Murphy's altruistic act on that day is remembered forever by Probyn, as without that help from the opposition physio, he may never been selected for England nor gone on to becoming one of England's finest tight head props, winning 37 caps, 2 grand slams and representing the World XV.

"Murphy's altruistic act on that day, is remembered forever by Probyn"

1988

A French telegram moments before an English Battle

The intense rivalry between England and France is renowned, particularly in the world of rugby. Some say this rivalry emanates from hundreds of years of wars. Some say it is just a cultural clash. Some say it is simply because both are often battling for the top spot in the Six Nations Championship. Whatever the reason it is sometimes ugly, often brutal and always intense.

However, English and French players united fleetingly in 1989 when a World XV was chosen to play against South Africa to celebrate the South African rugby centenary. The World Community began to soften its stance towards South Africa's apartheid government as it saw progressive improvements and continual changes occurring in the fight to remove apartheid from South Africa.

This is a once in a lifetime opportunity to take part in one of rugby unions rarer and more glamorous fixtures. Four English players, Winterbottom, Rendall, Teague & Probyn played alongside the best of the best drawn from France, Ireland, Wales, Scotland, New Zealand and Australia. So French and Englishmen battled together and friendships were made. The brief comaraderie ended and the players returned to their home countries.

Two years later, England travelled to France to play a big Six Nations match. When the England team arrived at their hotel, a telegram was waiting for the four English players who had played in the World XV. It was from the French captain, Pierre Berbizier, wishing all four players 'good luck' and reminding them to 'play the ball, ball, ball' (as he used to say during their brief tour).

Pierre Berbizier, captain of France and a true sportsman
Photograph PA Photos

Camaraderie, sportsmanship and civility exists between players who have total respect for each other, even in the gladiatorial battleground of an England v France Six Nations match as demonstrated by Berbizier's magical telegram.

"Camaraderie, sportsmanship and civility exists between players even in the gladiatorial battleground...as demonstrated by Berbizier's magical telegraph."

1989

Mayo man shows gentle kindness amidst an epileptic rugby moment

In the 1980s the London Irish Rugby Football Club fielded eleven teams every Saturday. Some felt that the 7th team, The Nomads, was the best winning team in the club. They played open (attacking) rugby and yet were as hard as nails.

It was a team full of good players, either top players on their way down from first team careers or young talent on their way up. Many never got past the Nomads as they became attracted to the fierce yet flowing brand of rugby which this team played.

Year after year they topped the win ratios as many talented players found themselves mesmerized by the style of the team both on and off the pitch. One young Kiwi, Warren Flavell, who had represented his province and was tipped by some to go all the way to representing his native New Zealand, took a year off and ended up playing for London Irish Nomads. That was it. He, like so many around him, decided to stay put on this team for many years.

Another young talented full back, known here as 'Rory', had made a similar decision. After a particularly engaging match, he came back into the dressing room after yet another fine victory and suddenly collapsed on the floor. He was having an epileptic fit. One of the players checked he hadn't swallowed his tongue. As he lay there in the recovery position, another player, one of the hardest players, yet kindest people, Johnny Mullarky, quietly asked the rest of the players to move to the next dressing room so that when Rory eventually woke up he wouldn't be embarrassed by everyone staring at him.

A soft subtle moment of kindness from a battle hardened 'salt of the earth' rugby hooker.

John Mullarky, London Irish RFC a hard man
with a big heart
Photograph Ze Zook

**" He quietly asked the rest of the players
to move to the next dressing room so
that Rory wouldn't be embarrassed
by everyone staring at him."**

1992

Derek Redmond's dad, Barcelona Olympic Games

Derek Redman was ready. His Olympic moment had arrived. The British 400 metre sprinter was fancied by many to win a medal (possibly gold) in Barcelona 1992. As a young world class athlete, he dreamt of winning a medal in the Olympic Games. When he was 19 he shattered the British 400 metre record. Then in 1988, he went to the 1988 Games in Seoul and just ten minutes before his race he had to withdraw with an Achilles tendon injury. He patiently waited, trained and prepared for four long years – for Barcelona '92.

He was in fine form and even though it was only the semi finals stage, he felt his moment had arrived.

The gun fired and Redmond ran beautifully, then broke from the pack and stormed into the lead. 65,000 fans and millions of TV viewers watched, what is the most difficult of all the track events – a non stop sprint for 400 metres. With 175 metres to go he heard a 'pop' from his right leg. His world imploded. He had pulled his right hamstring. He hobbled and fell to the track in total and utter despair. Derek's Dad, Jim, immediately ran from his seat towards the track to help his son.

Alone and lonely, Derek lay distraught on the track. He then rejected the offer of a stretcher, stood up and started hobbling onwards to complete the race. The other runners, by now, had already completed the race. The crowd slowly realized a very personal contest was unfolding before their eyes. He wasn't dropping out. He was finishing on one leg.

An Olympian struggle - Derek Redman and his Dad
at the Barcelona Games
Photograph PA Photos

The crowd started to clap and cheer him on. Meanwhile Derek Redman's Dad managed to jink past officials and get onto the track and catch up with his son 120 metres from the finish line. "I'm here, son," said Jim and he put his arm around his son. "We'll finish together." Derek burst into tears but the two kept running, kept hobbling towards the finish line.

65,000 people cheered and clapped them on. A few feet from the line Jim let go of his son so Derek could cross the line on his own. All of the 65,000 continued cheering and many wept as they were part of these very personal heart wrenching sporting moments.

"He stood up and started hobbling onwards to complete the race.....the crowd slowly realized a very personal contest was unfolding before their eyes."

1994

Norwegian Gold Medallist's opens Eritrea window to a whole new world

Johann Olav Koss was about to become an Olympic world champion speed skater when he travelled to Eritrea, the tiny country which had been liberated from Ethiopia. He saw children deprived of the right to play. The children couldn't be children. They had little safe space and no footballs. He decided to use his talents not just to win medals but to bring hope and help to those less fortunate than he. He would use his Olympic platform to publicise the plight of these children and the Olympic Aid's mission to help them.

Within a few months, Johann was back home and ready for the 1994 Winter Olympic Games. He was very very fast and very very focused – on two goals – winning medals and winning help for the Eritrean children.

He won gold medals at 1,500m, 5,000m and 10,000m races. He also set new world records in all three events. He now attracted the media and with that he managed to achieve his second goal – raising awareness and funds for Eritrean children.

Sports illustrated made him Sportsman of the Year in 1994. He also received the Oscar Mathisen Award in 1990, 1991 and 1994 and

Norwegian speed skater Johann Olav Koss on
his way to winning medals and helping thousands of
underprivileged kids
Photograph PA Photos

later went on be a a UNICEF ambassador. Koss
is now the CEO of the International Humanitarian
Organisation, Right To Play. Headquartered in
Toronto, its programmes help under privileged

children in 23 countries by using sport to teach children about teamwork, fair play, conflict resolution, self-esteem, communication, commitment, respect, and integrity.

Right To Play 'uses sports as a way to teach. Right To Play is committed to improving the lives of children and to strengthening their communities by translating the best practices of sport and play into opportunities to promote development, health and peace'.

"...using sport to teach children about teamwork, fair play, conflict resolution, self-esteem, communication, commitment, respect, and integrity."

Children's Charity: Right To Play www.righttoplay.com

1994

Dan the Determined Man fulfils his dying sister's promise – Lillehammer

Dan Jansen was a very fast speed skater destined, many felt for great things. Inspired by his sister Jane, Dan started skating at 16 and within a few years he was representing the USA in the 84 Sarajevo Olympic Games. He came 4th in the 500 metres. Four years later he was favourite to win in Calgary '88.

In the early hours of the morning of the race, Dan received a phone call to tell him his sister was dying of Leukaemia. He spoke to his sister, although she was not able to speak back to him. He promised her he would win the race for her. She died later that morning. He still took part in the 500 metre race but fell early on. A few days later he fell again in the 1000 metre race. He left Calgary empty handed and broken hearted, although he was awarded the US Olympic Spirit Award for his 'valiant efforts through tragedy'.

He waited and trained patiently for the next Olympic Games to come around. Alberta, France 1992 was soon upon him. Having broken the world record the year before, he was the hot favourite. Sadly, he finished fourth in the 500 metres and 26th in the 1,000 metres and left France empty handed.

At the age of 29, Dan knew that the 1994 Winter Olympic Games was his last chance to win an Olympic medal. Incidentally, this is the only time that the Winter Games have been held within two years of the preceding Summer Games.

US speed skater Dan Jansen finally took gold and fulfilled his promise to his dying sister
Photograph PA Photos

So he travelled to Lillehammer, Norway in search of the elusive Olympic medal and carrying the weight of his promise to his dead sister. Despite being the fastest in the world at 500 metres, he finished 8th. It seemed as if destiny was not going to allow him a medal. As he stepped up for his final event, the 1,000 metres, one wonders what thoughts went through his head. He won it, smashed the world record and took gold. He dedicated his gold medal to his sister Jane who had inspired him all those years ago.

During his victory lap, he carried his daughter with him around the ice. Her name was also Jane.

"During his victory lap, he carried his daughter with him around the ice. Her name was also Jane."

1995

Nelson Mandela, calms the rage and boosts the strength 1995

In the final few minutes before the kick off of the 1995 Rugby World Cup Final the South African team dressing room was at boiling point. The mood in the dressing room was ramped up to the point that the players were in danger of exploding on the pitch and losing their discipline. The captain, Francois Pienaar later said he was finding it difficult to keep the rage under control. The atmosphere was so intense

Then suddenly the dressing room door opened and in walked their new president, Nelson Mandela dressed in a South African rugby shirt. The players seemed to find a certain calmness from his presence and pride in their president wearing their beloved national rugby shirt. After wishing each player well, Mandela left the dressing room and a sense of calm combined with a new steely determination fell across the room. The South African team went out and beat the New Zealanders in an intense rugby world cup final.

For the first time the whole of South Africa was totally united. All races and religions were hugging each other. Pienaar said that, after the game, when President Mandela presented him with the cup, President Mandela said "Thank you very much for what you've done for South Africa.

" Pienaar said   "thank you for what you've done."

President Mandela presents South Africa's Francois
Pienaar the Rugby World Cup 1995
Photograph PA Photos

**"The mood in the dressing room was
ramped up to the point that the players were
in danger of exploding on the pitch and
losing their discipline."**

1996

Englishman saves Frenchman and loses his dream

Englishman Peter Goss had a dream. To win one of the world's great yachting challenges - the Vendée Globe non-stop, single- handed, round-the-world race. He had begged and borrowed and waited and finally got sponsors. He had a uniquely designed, world-class boat. He finally had a real chance to sail, and win, the 1996 race. Although he was up against much bigger and better funded yachts, he was going well in this year-long race.

It was Christmas Day when he received a distress call from a French competitor. He sent what could have been his last fax to his wife, telling her that he was turning his boat around to search for the Frenchman. He turned his 50-ft yacht, the Aqua Quorum, back into a hurricane- force headwind to attempt to rescue his competitor, French sailor Raphael Dinelli. Goss was risking his life and simultaneously abandoning his chance of winning the race. The Aqua Quorum was the first British yacht to enter the Vendée. Only 6 of the 16 starters actually finished the race. Two sailors had already lost their lives in 1996.

He battled 80mph winds and huge waves in the notoriously hostile Southern Ocean to eventually find the 'near dead' Dinellli, stiff and suffering from hypothermia as he had been freezing in a life raft for two days and nights. Goss nursed him with tea and physiotherapy and on New Year's Eve they toasted the future with a bottle of champagne that Dinelli had the foresight to bring. Dinelli also asked Goss if he could use his fax machine to propose to his girlfriend, who duly accepted and Peter Goss was best man.

Frenchman Raphael Dinelli sits in the cockpit of his yacht Algimouss on Nov. 2, 1996, on the eve of the start of the Vendee Globe Challenge and the soon to be near disaster
Photograph PA Photos

Dinelli and Goss became close friends and also vowed to sail together. They subsequently did so in the 1997 Transatlantic Jacques Vabre Race, going on to win in their class.

Round-the-World lone sailor, Peter Goss waves to the
crowds who turned out to meet him
Photograph PA Photos

Pete Goss was awarded France's highest honour, the Legion d'Honneur and he was also
awarded an MBE in Britain's 1998 New Year's
Honour List.

**"He turned his 50-ft yacht, the Aqua
Quorum, back into a hurricane – force headwind to attempt to rescue his competitor"**

1997

Scouser Fowler, protests against being awarded a penalty

Liverpool striker Robbie Fowler amidst the heat of an intense Arsenal v Liverpool top of the table clash, protested against the referee's decision to award him a penalty. Although he had fallen to the ground in the penalty box, he had not been tackled by the Arsenal Keeper, David Seaman. The referee, Gerald Ashby, pointed to the penalty spot. Fowler appealed to the referee to change his decision, without success.

Arsenal's goalkeeper gets his hand to Robbie Fowler's (far left) penalty kick at Highbury only to lose the ball to Jason McAteer (far right) who subsequently scored
Photograph PA Photos

Fowler was forced to take the penalty. Some say Fowler then took the penalty half- heartedly with a tame shot which, needless to say, the Arsenal keeper saved, but as the ball rebounded, Jason McAteer pounced and drove it home for a Liverpool goal.

Fowler's honesty could have been costly for Liverpool. However goals from Liverpool's Collymore and McAteer ensured that 'everyone was a winner'.

Fowler was later awarded the UEFA Fair Play Award and the FIFA General Secretary stated "Your reaction in the penalty incident...did you great honour. It is the kind of reaction which helps maintain the dignity of the game."

"It is the kind of reaction which helps maintain the dignity of the game."

1998

Never mind the war – there's honour in the battle USA v Iran World Cup

After cutting off diplomatic relations, the idea of Iran playing against the USA seemed surreal. In fact it was their first time ever playing each other and it was in the World Cup Finals 1998.

Fans mingled before, during and after the game as the fellowship of football prevailed.

Iranian Players (dark shirts) & USA Players (white shirts)
arm in arm united in the celebration of football
Photograph PA Photos

Before the game, the Iranian team gave bouquets of flowers to the American team who reciprocated with American souvenir badges.

Throughout the game, players helped each other off the ground, in fact the game was played in such a sporting manner that UEFA gave both teams its Fair Play award.

Iran won 2-1. Football had helped relations between the two countries. This was the start of a new relationship. Behind the scenes, both teams met the night before the game and agreed that this should be the start of a sporting relationship.

They met the day after the game and US Soccer then invited the Iranian team to play a three game tour of the United States. However, when the Iranians heard that upon entry all players would be finger printed and photographed, they objected. The USA State Department waived the regulation and the tour went ahead. USA and Iran drew 1-1.

The ISP reported comments captured the continuing moment: 'Football has again helped to heal wounds between two nations who twenty years ago seemed set to bleed forever.'

"After cutting off diplomatic relations, the idea of Iran playing against the USA seemed surreal."

1998

Modern Australian refuses to knock noble Australian Knight's record

Sir Donald Bradman is considered by many to be the world's greatest cricketer. He almost scored 1,000 runs (973) during the eight innings on Australia's 1930 tour. He also, once scored 334 runs in a single innings. Although Sir Don was arguably the world's best cricketer, he was a humble man. He has been described as an example of human kindness, honesty, integrity and virtue. In some ways his 'normality' made him all the more respected.

He had unwavering concentration for long periods. He was extremely exciting to watch because of the speed with which he scored runs (he once scored 309 runs in one day). He was a true gentleman - immaculately behaved and steeped in humility with a strong belief in sportsmanship, which in itself made him very special.

There is an old piece of Pathe News archive showing Bradman practising with a golf ball and a cricket stump. He hits the golf ball with the stump and hits it again on the rebound, time after time.

He scored almost 7,000 test runs, including 29 centuries. No other cricketer has even come close to his batting average of 99.94 over 52 test matches. He was only 4 runs short of averaging 100 when he picked up his bat for the last time in England in 1948. He was tragically bowled out for a duck. [See 1948 A Sad Celebration, A Standing Ovation and Three Cheers from the Opposition.] He was knighted in 1949 and went on to serve Australian cricket as chairman of Australia's cricket selectors. He was also a respected writer on cricket. He passed away in 2001 at the age of 92.

Aussie captain, Mark Taylor, was having none of it
Photograph PA Photos

Some three years prior to Sir Donald's death, Mark Taylor led his Australian team to Pakistan to their first victory in that country in 39 years. In the second Test at Peshawar, Taylor batted heroically for two days. At the end of second day's play he had scored 334 runs, equalling Sir Donal Bradman's record. Everyone including his team mates, the media and the fans wanted him to break the record and go on to break Brian Lara's new record of 375 runs. A massive crowd arrived the next day to see play resume.

Taylor was having none of it, and declared the innings closed. He opted to share the record with Sir Donald and simultaneously, improve the team's chances of winning the test. He was later widely praised for this decision. The Test ended in a draw. The third and final test also ended in a draw giving Australia the series.

"Everyone including his team mates, the media and the fans wanted him to break the record....
Taylor was having none of it..."

1999

French philosopher creates a New Rule when offering an English FA Cup rematch

The unwritten code of honour in many sports is to stop play when a player is seriously injured. In football, a team will kick a ball out of play to stop the game. In acknowledgement of that sporting gesture, the opposition normally resume play by throwing the ball to a team mate who promptly kicks the ball back to the opposition. Spectators appreciate this unwritten code of honour and usually a gentle appreciative applause ripples around the stadium.

For more than 100 years the FA Cup has generated many unique situations. In 1999 during a 5th round match between Arsenal (the holders) and Sheffield United, a United player, Lee Morris, was injured. His team mate kicked the ball out of play so Morris could receive treatment. After treatment, Arsenal's Ray Parlour threw the ball towards Sheffield United's goalkeeper, Alan Kelly. However Arsenal's debutant, Kanu, intercepted the ball, passed it to another Arsenal player, Marc Overmars, who went on to score what was deemed to be a dishonourable goal. Kanu was not aware that a Sheffield player was injured. Arsenal won 2-1. Sheffield United were outraged.

Arsenal were embarrassed. Arsenal's French

With arms outstretched and crowd behind him Arsenal's
sporting Frenchman, Arsene Venger
Photograph Arsenal FC

manager, Arsene Wenger, graciously offered
United's manager, Steve Bruce, a replay.

Bruce accepted. The FA agreed within an hour and the game was declared void (although the yellow cards issued during the game remained valid). Although FIFA's president, Sepp Blatter, praised the gesture, FIFA decided it had to discuss the issue, since no laws had been broken by Kanu – he had only contravened an unwritten rule of sportsmanship.

FIFA allowed the game to be replayed. 10 days after the original game, they famously replayed each other. Arsenal won 2-1 again.

"Arsenal's manager, graciously offered a replay. Steve Bruce accepted"

2001

Sailing teams refuse to sail until opposition ready

Four-fifths of the gruelling Atlantic yacht race were complete. The contestants EDS Atlantic Challenge had all made it safely through the first four stages. With the final leg scheduled to start on the Monday at 1700 BST, the leader, Sill Plein Fruit, still needed critical repairs to its mast. There simply wasn't enough time to fix the mast before the scheduled restart on Monday. A meeting between the race organizers and all of the contestants was held. Race organizer, Sir Chay Blyth, said that there was a unanimous vote to delay the final stage to allow repairs to the leader's yacht.

The contestants felt that the race was not the same without 'the big red boat' that had led throughout all four stages.

Nick Moloney, the skipper of Kingfisher (who went on to eventually win the race) was delighted with the decision from all of the contestants. "It shows once again the unity felt by the teams in this race. We're really happy."

Sill had led the race throughout but had damaged its mast during the fourth leg. In fact it was still sailing into Boston harbour with its damaged mast, when the meeting was held and the decision announced.

French yachtsman Roland Jourdain poses aboard his
monohull "Sill et Veolia" Friday

Photograph PA Photos

The race was finally won by Kingfisher who surprised everyone (almost catching out the waiting spectators and race officials) as they emerged from the mist and sailed over the finishing line in St. Malo, France. Within a couple of miles came the nearest two contenders, Sill Plein Fruit and Ecover.

EDS Challenge final positions
1. Kingfisher 38 points
2. Sill Plein Fruit 31 pts
3. Ecover 30 pts
4. Gartmore 26 pts
5. Fila 14 pts

Roland Jourdain, the skipper of the Sill Plein Fruit was extremely grateful to all of the competing skippers for agreeing to delay the final stage. "You would never see the Schumacher brothers making such a gesture. This goes to the heart of the EDS Atlantic Challenge and to the heart of professional sailing. It's why we love this sport so."

"There was a unanimous vote to delay the final stage to allow repairs to the leader's yacht."

2001

Swede refuses umpire's error to give Frenchman tennis victory

Top four seed Magnus Norman fancied his chances of getting into the quarter finals and possibly winning a tennis major as he was the last of the top four seeds left in the competition. The Swede was playing against the 16th seed Frenchman, Sebastien Grosjean in the fourth round of the Australian Open.

Frenchman Sebastien Grosjean
Photograph PA Photos

The Frenchman proved too good and got to match point. Grosjean served an ace to win the match. As the players were shaking hands, the umpire announced the last serve was a 'let' (the ball had supposedly hit the net and therefore the 'match point' needed to be retaken). The net machine recorded it as a 'let'. Both players felt the machine was wrong and that the serve was, in fact, a legitimate ace. Amidst this late-night drama, the Swede refused the umpire's invitation to replay the point and gave the Frenchman the match.

Norman explained "There was no let. I didn't want to take the point. If I had taken it, the match could have turned around and I would have felt bad. When I leave the court and go home I want to feel good about myself."

The Frenchman appreciated the gesture of honesty and later said of Magnus Norman "He's a nice guy, never trying to cheat or anything like that."

"The Swede refused the umpire's invitation to replay the point and gave the Frenchman the match."

133

2001

Italian Paulo Di Canio stops an English Premiership Game

West Ham's Italian striker Paolo Di Canio had a chance to shoot into an empty, gaping goal against Everton in 2001 as the opposition goalkeeper Paul Gerrard, lay injured on the ground outside his penalty area. Di Canio decided to catch the ball with his hands instead of scoring and thereby stopping play so that Gerrard could get treatment.

Everton fans packed into Goodison Park knew they were witnessing a magical moment of sportsmanship. The game ended in a 1-1 draw. Football Authority FIFA described Di Canio's gesture as a "special act of good sportsmanship" and subsequently awarded Di Canio the Fifa Fair Play award – football's highest honour for sportsmanship.

This was an example of how someone who has made mistakes can, if given a chance, improve and act in the most honourable way – Di Canio had previously been banned for pushing referee Paul Alcock to the floor in 1998 when he was playing for Sheffield Wednesday.

Di Canio did say, "Only stupid people would say I was wrong, and that we could be in sixth place if it wasn't for me. I was definitely right to do what I did. Sometimes you have to think about situations very quickly. Even if my mother and father told me I was wrong, I would disagree.

"The players and the manager have said nothing to me. They are intelligent and know why I caught the ball.

"I have never been in that situation before, but I would be lying if I could tell you how I would react if it had happened in a World Cup Final." Di Canio was, without doubt, one of the most talented footballers to grace British Football – he is also fondly remembered in Celtic FC (Scotland) where they still sing ballad songs about his unique skills and the total joy of football which he relentlessly expressed.

Di Canio scored many goals – this one against Chelsea
Photograph PA Photos

"Only stupid people would say I was wrong, and that we could be in sixth place if it wasn't for me."

2001

Teenage Ghanaian, Sumaila Abdallah gives Kiss Of Life

A young man with an old head is how Ghana's footballer Sumalla Abdallah could be described. How many 19 year old footballers would know what to do if they saw another player collapse? Sumalla Abdallagh did. In fact, the young goalkeeper's quick thinking and knowledge of first aid saved an opponent's life.

As Charles Taylor fell down, and stayed down, Sumaila ran over to him as he sensed he was in danger. He revived Charles by giving him mouth-to-mouth resuscitation

The sensitivity and quick reaction of Abdallah saved a fellow footballer's life. In fact his initial interest in learning about mouth-to-mouth resuscitation demonstrated a certain selflessness.

Sumaila Abdallah was consequently awarded FIFA's Fair Play diploma in 2001. He went on to say that "Winning a Fair Play diploma, at age 19, will motivate me in my football career. And I hope to win more honours for myself and Ghana."

"...the young goalkeeper's quick thinking and knowledge of first aid saved an opponent's life."

2001

American Lance Armstrong beats cancer & wins 7 Tour De France

"Without cancer, I never would have won a single Tour de France. Cancer taught me a plan for more purposeful living, and that in turn taught me how to train and to win more purposefully. It taught me that pain has a reason, and that sometimes the experience of losing things–whether health or a car or an old sense of self–has its own value in the scheme of life. Pain and loss are great enhancers." Forbes Magazine December 3, 2001.

Lance Armstrong had already won three Tours de France when he made this statement. He went on to win another four. In 2002, Sports Illustrated awarded him Sportsman of the Year. In 2003 he was awarded the BBC International Sports Personality Of The Year. In that same year he was also awarded ESPN's ESPY Award for Best Male Athlete in the same year and again in 2004, 2005 and 2006.

When he was diagnosed with cancer he had a 3% chance of survival – although some doctors told him he had a 40% chance. He survived testicular cancer, a germ cell tumour that metastasized to his brain and lungs in 1996. He underwent brain and testicular surgery and chemotherapy. Then he went on to win the world's toughest race, the Tour De France in 1999. He repeated this in 2000, 2001, 2002, 2003, 2004 and 2005.

American Lance Armstrong, 7 times winner of
the Tour de France
Photograph PA Photos

By the time he retired in 2005, he had won the Tour de France seven consecutive times (beating Miguel Indurain's record of five consecutive wins) from 1999 through to 2005.

He now helps other cancer sufferers through Live Strong – the Lance Armstrong Foundation www.livestrong.org

"It taught me that pain has a reason, and that sometimes the experience of losing things ....has its own value in the scheme of life."

See 2003 Cycling's Gentleman's Club Wait For Leader To Remount for more on Lance Armstrong

2002

Millwall stand still and watch Bournemouth score

Millwall football club has a hard reputation. Nevertheless they are a club who believe in sportsmanship and that 'fair play must prevail'. In 2002, Milwall FC's reserves played Bournemouth reserves in the Avon Insurance Combination.

As is the honourable tradition in football, when a player is injured the ball is kicked out of play to allow treatment. Consequently the team who restart the game pass the ball back to the opposition – usually the goal keeper.

When two of Bournemouth's players, Ryan Woolfenden and Danny Thomas accidentally collided, the ball was kicked out of play by Bournemouth to allow the players to receive treatment. When both players had recovered, Milwall resumed by sportingly giving possession to Bourenmouth by passing the ball to the Bournemouth goal for its French goal keeper, Michael Menetrier. However the keeper wasn't expecting the ball at that moment as he was out of his goal, and the ball agonizingly trickled over the line for a goal.

Affectionately known as the Lions, Millwall FC could not accept such a goal. In immediate agreement with the coach, Joe McLaughlin, the Millwall team, to a man, stood still while

Millwall FC – The Lions with a big heart
Photograph Brian Tonks

Bournemouth took the restart kick-off from the halfway line. Millwall's eleven players silently watched as the Bournemouth striker, Amos Foyewa, was allowed a free run to effectively walk the ball into the Millwall goal. With the scores now equal, hand shakes were exchanged and the real game recommenced. Milwall went on to win 2-1.

"Millwall's eleven players silently watched as the Bournemouth striker was allowed a free run to effectively walk the ball into the Millwall goal."

See 1999 French Philospher Wenger and Di Canio 2001.

2003

Cycling's gentlemen's club wait for leader to remount

Amidst the intensity of one of the world's toughest sports – the Tour de France - America's cycling hero Lance Armstrong collided with a spectator. His competitors, including his arch rival Jan Ullrich, stopped and waited for the American to get up and remount.

Cycling has an unwritten code of honour amongst the professional cyclists, despite the negative publicity the sport receives about the misuse of performance enhancing drugs. There is a long held tradition of sportsmanship in the Tour de France.

Two years previously, in 2001, the arch rivals Armstrong and Ullrich were racing head to head as they rapidly descended the Col de Peyresourde in the Pyrenees when Ullrich crashed on a corner. Armstrong waited to see if the German was ok and proceeded to coast slowly while Ullrich remounted and restarted.

The unwritten code of honour applies to a variety of situations including punctures or calls of nature that happen to the yellow jersey (leader of a particular stage) or to any of the leading cyclists.

Cyclists cannot assume the race will stop, as

(L-R) Lance Armstrong crashes along with
Iban Mayo as Jan Ullrich swerves to avoid them and
then waits for them to remount.
Photograph PA Photos

sometimes in the mayhem of an accident some
cyclists manage to avoid the crash and continue
on without perhaps being fully aware. However
overall the unwritten code of honour prevails,
and it is this that arguably makes the peloton (the
main group of riders in the race) so special.

Although the peloton was once called the 'con-
victs of the road' the contestants honour an
unwritten rule of sportsmanship that few, if any,

sports adhere to as the hardened Tour de France cyclists have a common understanding of sportsmanship.

"The unwritten code of honour applies to a variety of situations including punctures or calls of nature that happen to the yellow jersey."

See 2001 American Lance Armstrong Beats Cancer & Wins 7 Tour De France

2004

Accrington Stanley's Paul Cook relives Eusebio's honour

The FA Cup has a long and colourful history. It attracts huge overseas television audiences. It has its own magic. Possibly because it delivers the most romantic of shocks, with underdogs somehow beating big clubs year in year out at various stages - including the Cup Final itself. In 2004 Accrington Stanley FC (part-timers) were taking on the professionals from Colchester FC in the third round of FA Cup.

Accrington Stanley FC (part-timers) –
the club that wouldn't die
Photograph Kipax.com

In a sublime moment, during the final seconds of the game, Accrington Stanley's Paul Cook rose to Rory Prendergast's perfect free-kick to head home a certain goal from point-blank range. Cook, a former Wolves and Burnley player, knew it was goal-bound and felt a beautiful FA Cup shock coming on as non league Accrington were going to cause another magical FA Cup shock by knocking out the professional big boys from Colchester FC.

Out of nowhere, the Colchester keeper, Simon Brown, somehow got his hand to the ball and pushed it away. Within seconds Cook's disbelief turned to disappointment and then to admiration for this extraordinary save. With a smile, he wrapped his arms around the Colchester goal-keeper and congratulated him. "What are you doing to us?" Cook asked Brown during that magical moment of sportsmanship.

Brown said later "I hadn't met Paul before but he's a top man. All the lads in the dressing-room have nice things to say about him."

The match ended 0–0 with the replay set for 7 days later. Colchester won the replay 2-1.

"He wrapped his arms around the Colchester goalkeeper and congratulated him."

Acrington Stanley's true sportsman, Paul Cook,
trudges off after feeling a beautiful FA Cup shock for a
split second.
Photograph Kipax.com

*See 1968 Eusebio's applause for the opposition
goal keeper*

2004

Tackled & bruised by Irish priest, Brazilian Marathon runner runs on

In the lead, running the race of his life in the ultimate race, the Marathon, in the ultimate event, the Olympic Games, Brazil's Vanderlei Cordeiro de Lima was looking good. He had a 48 second lead at the 35 km (21.75 miles) mark and with less than 10 km (6.2 miles) to finish, he could see a gold medal within his sights as he pounded the streets of Athens. Suddenly a spectator lept out of the crowd, grabbed de Lima, threw him into the crowd and onto the ground.

In those few horrifying seconds, two competitors caught up and overtook de Lima. Spectators grappled with the intruder, a defrocked priest, Cornelius Horan (who had previously lept onto a Formula 1 racing track and proceeded to dance an Irish jig). The destraught de Lima picked himself up, gritted his teeth and somehow continued the race (he lost the gold medal, but did manage to win bronze as well as the hearts and sympathies of every sports lover worldwide).

De Lima's winning position was no fluke. He had won gold at the Pan American games in 1999 (Winnipeg) and 2003 (Santo Domingo).

He was in great form and racing the race of his life. He was aiming to be Brazil's first marathon gold medallist. The whole of Brazil held its breath

Defrocked Irish priest Cornelius Horan, right, grabs
Vanderlei de Lima of Brazil and knocks him into the
crowd during the men's Marathon event at the 2004
Olympic Games in Athens
Photograph PA Photos

as he held his lead with six miles to go. And then
his dream was snatched away from him. He did
not, however, give up.

He got up heroically and continued the race.
Vandrlei always maintained that his humble
origins and the constant struggle to work to get
enough money to buy rice and beans actually
prepared him to be a good marathon runner.

Perhaps it also prepared him for this terrible struggle in Athens which would have destroyed many other runners.

He ran on and even managed a little victory dance during the last seconds of the race which he completed in third place. The Brazilian Track Federation appealed for a gold medal as their runner had been taken out of the race but the appeal that 'solutions like that have been done in the past' was rejected. He was given bronze medal but he was also awarded the Pierre de Couberin medal for Sportsmanship at the closing event.

This special sportsmanship medal was officially presented to him in December in Rio de Janeiro, where he was also named named "Brazilian Athlete Of The Year" (2004) which was chosen, for the first time by an online popular vote. In July 2005 the Brazilian beach volleyball player, Emanuel Rego presented his own Olympic gold medal (Athens 2004) to Vanderli on TV, who - although deeply moved - returned the medal. He said "I can't accept Emanuel's medal. I'm happy with mine, it's bronze but means gold."

"His humble origins and the constant struggle to work to barely get enough money to buy rice and beans, actually prepared him to be a good marathon runner."

2005

Australian Warne applauds Englishman in the Heat of Battle

There is a history of intense rivalry between England and Australia when it comes to cricket. During the 2005 Ashes series between England and Australia at Edgbaston, Birmingham, England, the cameras caught a private moment of sportsmanship.

Although Australia's Shane Warne enjoyed winning,
he also appreciated and applauded the opposition
Photograph PA Photos

Australia's record holding spin bowling star, Shane Warne, was caught on camera shouting repeatedly after England's batsmen Andrew Flintoff as he walked off. Warne shouted five or six times after Flintoff to congratulate him on his excellent innings.

Flintoff, despite carrying an injury, had indeed batted brilliantly. England went on to beat Australia in the Ashes series for the first time since 1987 by eventually going on to draw the final Test at The Oval on Monday.

"Warne shouted five or six times after Flintoff to congratulate him on his excellent innings."

2006

The unique goalkeepers' union – Iranian sympathy for his Mexican brother

Personal tragedy struck the Mexican goalkeeper Sanchez, during the 2006 World Cup Finals in Germany. His father, Felipe, died suddenly and most unexpectedly (from a heart attack) in Guadalajara on the Thursday. With the permission of his team, the sad Sanchez made the long and lonely journey across the world to bury his beloved father. Leaving behind the euphoria of playing in the World Cup Finals, Sanchez knew he might never play in another World Cup Match.

The team didn't know if he'd make it back for the game on the Sunday.

He did. He buried his father and spent time grieving with his family before they insisted he get back on the plane and flew across the world in time to play in game against Iran on the Sunday.

As is the tradition in big international football matches, after the national anthems, the players file past each other shaking hands. The two goalkeepers are usually at the end of the line. When the goalkeepers met, the Iranian keeper paused and bent down to pick up a bouquet of flowers which he gave to his opposite number, Sanchez the Mexican goalkeeper.

Although Mexico went on to win 3-1, the goal-keepers' moment transcended politics, power and even football results and demonstrated that from the brotherhood of sport, to the brotherhood of football, to the brotherhood of those unique people – goalkeepers, great sportsmanship prevails.

The brotherhood of football transcends all as demonstrated by the beautiful gesture from the Iranian goalkeeper to the Mexican goalkeeper
Photograph PA Photos

"When the goalkeepers met, the Iranian keeper paused and bent down to pick up a bouquet of flowers which he gave to his opposite number"

2006

American golfer, Tom Lehman offers a prayer for opponent's wife

At the US PGA Golf Championship in the Medinah Country Club Chicago, America's Ryder Cup golf captain, Tom Lehman, invited fellow professional to a private prayer for his golf friend and Ryder Cup opposition Darren Clarke whose wife, Heather, had passed away a short time earlier. It was 6.30 am and before the day's golf started. Some of the world's finest golfers took quiet time to pray and reflect in the early morning. The captain led a prayer for one of his opposition.

2006 US Ryder Cup captain, Tom Lehman
shared his opposition's grief
Photograph PA Photos

Soon he would wage battle against Clarke and the European team in golf's most prestigious event, the Ryder Cup. A competition where the best of Europe compete with the best the USA. Golfers play for each other instead of for money. It is unique in so far as these professional players don't get paid. They play for the honour and glory of the famous Ryder Cup.

America eventually lost to Europe in Ireland's K Club. During his captain's closing remarks, Lehman made a magnificent speech. He also acknowledged another magical sporting moment when Irishman Paul McGinley gave an American rookie a 'gimme' putt (see next page).

"The captain lead a prayer for one of his opposition."

See 2006 Irishman Paul McGinley Saves American Rookie From Ryder Cup Embarrassment

2006

Irishman Clarke declines Leprechauns' help

On Sunday 24 May 2006, Irish Golfer Darren Clarke found his ball deep in thick rough grass on the 9th hole in Carlton Golf Club, County Kildare, Ireland. Effectively this would cost him one shot as all he could do was to hack out of the rough and onto the fairway a few yards away instead of shooting straight at the green. He was winning by two shots with 10 holes to play. Suddenly the hooter sounded which meant all players had to leave the course and suspend their matches because of bad weather.

When Clarke returned on Monday, he discovered that his ball magically now had an almost perfect lie as it sat on top of the somehow flattened thick grass. It was suggested that the leprechauns had been at work overnight − he could now shoot directly at the green and save himself a shot. So he asked for a ruling and Clarke was informed that he could play the ball in its improved position and he should thank the 'little people'!

37 year old Clarke felt bad as he knew that either the crowds of people had miraculously trodded down the grass all around the ball or indeed, the 'little people' had been at work. He chose not to take advantage and shoot for the green directly, but instead he played a short chip shot sideways onto the fairway − the same shot he would have

Darren Clarke chose to play an extra shot rather than
take an unfair advantage

had to play if he was still stuck in thick grass (effectively costing him an extra shot and narrowing his lead to just one shot). Clarke later explained in a BBC interview: "When I went back out the area around the ball had been flattened. It was a much better lie than when I left it. I could have put it on to the front of the green from where it was, but my conscience would not allow me to do it so I just decided the best thing to do was chip out like I would have done the previous night. Honesty is part and parcel of the game and I could not have acted any other way." A magnificent, noble gesture from a true sportsman.

"Honesty is part and parcel of the game and I could not have acted any other way."

2006

America's Phil Mickleson's embrace of Irish opposition Ryder Cup Golf

Tee-ing off in front a big crowd can be a daunting experience, even for an experienced profession-al. Tee-ing off on the first day of golf's greatest competition, the Ryder Cup, has to be even more daunting. Tee-ing off on day number one of the Ryder Cup when you are still grieving the death of your wife, must be extraordinarily tense.

The warmth of Phil Mickleson's welcome helped Darren Clarke to cope with his grief and go on to play fantastic golf
Photograph PA Photos

When Ireland's hugely talented, Darren Clarke, walked onto the first tee on the opening day of the Ryder Cup 2006 at the K Club, his opposite number, America's Phil Mickleson, walked towards him, held out his arms and embraced him in a warm bear hug.

A magical sporting moment for the world to see. The still grieving Clarke had lost his wife, Heather (39) to cancer only a month before and was probably a bag full of mixed emotions as he stepped up to the tee in the world's greatest golfing competition. The warmth and affection shown by his competitor helped to relax him and reassure him. Clarke hit a great shot.

In fact, Clarke went on to birdie his first hole and ultimately he and his partner Lee Westwood beat the Americans, Mickleson and DiMarco, on the first of three days of intense golf. Clarke held it together for his European golf team as they battled against the Americans during three days of highly competitive world class golf.

Mickleson's gesture helped Clarke to master his grief so that he could play his natural game – brilliant golf.

"...his opposite number, America's Phil Mickleson, walked towards him, held out his arms and embraced in a warm bear hug."

2006

Irishman McGinley saves American rookie from Ryder Cup embarrassment

In the heat of the 36th Ryder Cup, Ireland's Paul McGinley and American rookie JJ Henry were having a very close game right up the 18th hole.

McGinley hit a 3 wood to within 30 ft of the hole leaving himself a long putt for an eagle (to get down in 3 shots on a par 5 hole). McGinley then rolled his putt down to within one foot of the pin. Henry conceded the putt (gave it to McGinley so that he scored a birdie 4).

Henry now needed a 25 ft foot putt to get down in 4 shots and effectively halve the hole and draw the match. This was an important putt, because if he missed it, Henry would lose the match and America would suffer its worst ever defeat by Europe in the history of the Ryder Cup.

What happened next, only McGinley can describe as the TV cameras did not show it: "As I was walking off the green the streaker ran past me and I said to him 'Don't run on his line' as can be seen if you lip read from the TV footage. The thought of conceding his putt at that stage had not crossed my mind, however, as I got to the edge of the green and turned around to watch JJ putt I saw the streaker running around JJ in a circular motion, as JJ was crouched down to read

McGinley (R) concedes the putt and shakes hands with JJ Henry (L) with an unidentified flying object in the background
Photograph Getty Photos

the putt, and trampling on JJ's line. This was the stage that I realised that it would be unfair to ask JJ to putt as his line had been compromised by the streaker running over it several times. I then walked towards JJ and told him to pick up his ball as his putt was conceded."

Rather than allowing the rookie American to putt and probably miss and consequently lose the game, McGinley felt it was wrong for the young American to suffer such an indignity.

The American captain, Tom Lehman, saw this magical moment and mentioned it in his closing speech as a true moment of sportsmanship, at the 36th Ryder Cup in Ireland's magical K Club.

"McGinley chose not to allow the young American to suffer the indignity."

2006

Norwegian helps Canadian & loses medal Ski Sprint Turin

"In the eyes of Canadians, we took a silver medal, but Norway has won gold for sportsmanship." The following describes the extraordinary act which prompted such words.

Canadian sprint skier Sara Renner was struggling with a broken ski pole in the sprint final in the Turin Winter Olympic Games when suddenly the Norwegian head coach, Bjørnar Håkensmoen, handed her a lifeline – a new ski pole. Renner recovered and went on to win silver while the Norwegian finalist missed the medals by one place, finishing fourth.

Over 7,000 grateful Canadian fans subsequently started sending cans of Canada's best Maple Syrup to Håkensmoen. He was stunned by the response and later told the Associated Press "It was natural for me to do it, and I think anyone should have done it. I didn't think about it. It was just a reflex ... but the response has been unbelievable."

5.2 tons of maple syrup were eventually given to Håkensmoen at a ceremony in Oslo. Both the Norwegian and Canadian governments suspended their normal regulations and agreed to waive import duties which could have made the syrup too expensive to accept. The Norwegians ambassador to Canada, Tor Naess, said "I am surprised, for a Norwegian it was quite natural to hand over the pole, like we did there."

Canadians will forever love their Norwegian sporting hero. The feelings are summed up by the words used at the beginning of this story - taken from an email sent by Geoff Snow, of Waterford, Ont. to the Oslo newspaper Aftenposten: "In the eyes of Canadians, we took a silver medal, but Norway has won gold for sportsmanship ".

"Norway has won gold for sportsmanship"

2006

American Cheek provokes a Charitable Chain Reaction

In January 2006 William Joseph Cheek became the world speed skating sprint champion. Then in the Winter Olympic Games in Turin that same year, Cheek won the 500m race. At the post race press conference Cheek announced that he was donating his gold medal bonus ($25,000) to the underprivileged children's charity, Right To Play formed by Norwegian 1993 gold medallist Johann Olav Koss.

'Joey' then went on to challenge others to do likewise and make pledges to support the 'Right To Play'. He then also donated his silver medal prize money from the 1,000 metres race.

Since his donation others have joined in and over $390,000 has been contributed to this cause.

He inspired Canada's multi-sport medal winner Clara Hughes to give $10,000 from her own money, as Canada does not pay win bonuses (Hughes won Olympic medals at cycling and speed skating – see 2006).

William 'Joey' Cheek was was chosen by his US teammates to carry their National Flag into the closing ceremonies.

World speed skating champion, William 'Joey' Cheek,
donated his prize money to Right To Play
Photograph PA Photos

"He was donating his gold medal bonus ($25,000) to the underprivileged children's charity."

*See 1993 Norwegian Gold Medallist's Opens Eritrea
Window to a Whole new World*

*Note: Children's Charity: Right To Play
www.righttoplay.com*

2006

Canadian multi-medal winning Olympian supports 'Right To Play'

Clara Hughes is a rare breed of sportsperson – a cyclist and a speed skater. She is also an extremely successul sportsperson having won Olympic medals in both sports. She is now part of a unique club Summer & Winter Olympic Medal Winners – being the fourth person (and the second woman) to win in both Olympic seasons.

Hughes competed in the 1996 and 2000 Olympic Games and won two bronze medals for cycling in the 1996 Olympic Games (individual road race and the individual time trial). She then switched her focus to speed skating and qualified for the 2002 Winter Olympic Games and won bronze in the 5,000 metres. She went on to the 2006 Olympic Games and won her first gold medal in the 5,000 metres (and a silver medal in the women's team pursuit).

All in all, Clara Hughes won five Olympic medals spanning 10 years. Although Canadians do not receive win bonuses, Hughes did donate $10,000 of her own money to the underprivileged children's charity 'Right To Play' founded by Norwegian Gold medallist skater, Johann Olav Koss *(see 1994)* and more recently inspired by American Gold medal speed skater William Joseph Cheek *(see 2006)*.

Ciara Hughes won Olympic medals in cycling in 1996
and 2000 and speed skating in 2002 and 2006 and
donated personally to Right To Play
Photograph PA Photos

**"Although Canadians do not receive
win bonuses, Hughes did donate $10,000
of her own money to the undeprivileged
children's charity."**

2007

God Save Croke Park - sport prevails over Auld Enemy bitterness Dublin

When Ireland's hidden jewel in the crown, Croke Park Stadium, finally agreed to allow 'foreign games' such as rugby and soccer internationals to be played there whilst Lansdowne Road (the oldest international rugby ground in the world) was being refurbished, inevitably it caused controversy when England came to town.

Ireland's hidden jewel in the crown, Croke Park
Photograph PA Photos

When British troops, the notorious 'Black and Tans', along with police auxiliaries opened fire into the packed crowd in Croke Park in 1920, 14 people died. This infamous massacre was called 'Bloody Sunday'. Among the dead was Michael Hogan, a Tipperary player. The Hogan stand in Croke Park is named after him.

Naturally, the thought of the Irish Army band playing the English national anthem 'God Save The Queen' stirred deep emotions. One protestor withdrew his family's collection of GAA (Gaelic Athletic Association) medals which had been on loan to the Museum in Croke Park. However the family of murdered Michael Hogan accepted that the anthem should be played.

The GAA promotes Irish games – hurling (the fastest field game in the world) and Gaelic Football (a mixture of rugby and soccer). Founded in 1884, it promoted Irish games, culture and the language. In 1918 it was on the list of organisations banned by the occupying British forces.

One compromise suggested was to get the popular Irish band, the Saw Doctors, to play God Save the Queen (as they add some excitement to their songs and often use hurleys to hit tennis balls into the crowd at their concerts). The President of Ireland, Mary MacAleese, recalled that in 1973, during the height of the Troubles, it was England who agreed to play in Dublin when Scotland and Wales refused to travel. She asked

that on the day the English be given as big a welcome as they were given back then (an eight
minute standing ovation).

The Irish Times correspondent, Fintan O'Toole
reported "We are a sovereign nation with average per capita incomes above those of the UK,"
and he noted that the Irish should be "confident
and at ease in situations where we used to feel
Anglophobia". And indeed they could be with
82,300 tickets sold out many months earlier (and
some selling at £1,600).

England and Ireland lined up against each other in Croke
Park with Ireland going on to win by a record score
Photograph PA Photos

The people of Ireland showed dignity and mutu-
al respect for national difference. The English
were applauded as they ran onto the pitch. God

Save The Queen was sung without interruption. Then came the Irish national anthem "Amhrán na bhFiann" and its additional compromise song "Ireland's Call" which were sung with unprecedented passion by a packed house of more than 82,000. Several of the Irish players were seen on TV with tears rolling down their cheeks. Tears of pride gave way to whooping jubilation as Ireland ran in their biggest ever victory over England, 43-13.

Irish and Lions hero Ollie Campbell said, "I have never in my life been more proud to be an Irishman." It was indeed a great day for Irish sport. The entire occasion was one of the most memorable occasions ever witnessed. It was an act of sporting reconciliation. And it happened in Croke Park.

"It was an act of sporting reconciliation. And it happened in Croke Park."

See 1973 England's Rugby Captain, John Pullin – 'at least we turned up'

2007

The night the Beautiful Game returned

For Leicester City Football Club and Nottingham Forest Football Club, the Carling Cup represents a realistic target for winning a trophy. Many of the premier league sides do not play their strongest teams in this competition as they consider the premiere league and the FA Cup to be more attractive targets. Smaller, lower league clubs always feel they are in with a chance of actually winning this trophy and are therefore desperate to win. Both sides felt they were in with a chance of ultimately winning the Trophy. On top of this, these clubs are keen neighbouring rivals. BBC's Paul Grant described it as playing 'in the pressure-cooker of an East Midlands derby.'

Notts Forest were winning 1-0 when one of their young and talented players, Clive Clarke, collapsed with what turned out to be a heart attack. The match was immediately abandoned. The player survived. A replay date was set.

Leicester City felt that it was unfair for Notts Forest to lose the goal they had legitimately scored. However the rules of the competition state that a rematch is a rematch and therefore has to start 0-0. Leicester City represent all that is right with this beautiful game, so they allowed Notts Forest goalkeeper, Paul Smith, to walk the ball into the net unopposed to give Forest the

The pressure cooker of an East Midland's derby
Photograph PA Photos

Leicester equalized. Notts Forest scored again to go 2-1 up. Then with two minutes to go Leicester equalized. Finally with just seconds remaining Leicester scored the winner and progressed on to the third round.

Paul Grant's headline 'The night the beautiful game returned' seemed to capture the moment. He went on to say that "football, and its administrators, coaches and players, can still be galvanised in the face of adversity and follow the path of decency with comprehensive unity.

"That both clubs were, at different times, willing to jeopardise the promise of money, prestige and local bragging rights in favour of common courtesy and camaraderie on the field speaks volumes about the value of sportsmanship in a sport which many see as having suffered a moral degeneration in recent years. "Amidst this backdrop, the result of a 3-2 victory for Leicester almost pales into virtual insignificance. How often can we enjoy the luxury of saying that?"

Sportsman and manager Gary Megson:
'The idea came from the whole club'
Photograph Neil Plumb

"Both clubs were ... willing to jeopardise the promise of money, prestige and local bragging rights in favour of common courtesy and camaraderie"

2007

Hardman Johnson makes crowd weep for the Return of a Little Girl

When a three year old girl was stolen from her bed in a holiday apartment in Portugal, the world was sickened. Her parents, the McCanns, somehow kept the media spotlight on their missing daughter in the hope that someone, somewhere, would spot their daughter and report it to the police. Part of their campaign managed to work with sports clubs and associations including Everton FC, the Football Association, the Scottish Football Association, the Rugby Football Union, the European Rugby Cup (Heineken Cup) and the English Cricket Authority – where pictures of Madeline were displayed and, in the case of the England v West Indies test match, the players wore yellow ribbons.

Pictures of Madeleine's distinctive eyes (one eye's pupil bleeds into the iris) could be seen at the FA Cup final, the EUFA Cup Final in Glasgow and in Twickenham for the European Rugby Cup final.

The English World Cup Winning captain, Martin Johnson made an appeal to the assembled crowd on behalf of Madeline's parents. Johnson is a big man. He is a hard man who took no prisoners on the field of play. He is also world cup winning captain. However this giant of a man spoke so passionately about the three year old's plight that grown men were moved to tears in the crowd. A moment of utter kindness from an utterly hard man. In fact, one Munster fan later said that he'd never heard anything like it. Munster, incidentally were not in the final but many of their supporters were there having optimistically bought tickets many months in advance.

This picture of Madeleine's distinctive eyes (one eye's pupil bleeds into the iris) in Twickenham at the Heineken Cup Final
Photograph PA Photos

"A moment of utter kindness from an utterly hard man."

2007

Alan Johnston's Palestinian kidnapper's sporting kindness

BBC correspondent Alan Johnston was abducted in March 2007 in Palestine's (lawless) Gaza strip. He was the only international correspondent still working in Gaza. After five weeks an unknown militant group claimed they had killed him. In the same week, Christian, Muslim, Jewish representatives and many journalist gathered at St. Martin in the Fields, a well-known London church, and Alan's sister, Katriona Johnston, joined BBC Scotland staff for a vigil in Glasgow.

Palestinian supporters of the Popular Front for the Liberation of Palestine hold posters of kidnapped BBC correspondent Alan Johnston during a protest demanding his release in Gaza City
Photograph PA Photos

One day during his captivity, Alan was suddenly told to leave his room and as he walked down a corridor, he thought this was it. This was the end, and that, finally, they were going to shoot him. Then he thought no, they're going to torture me. He feared torture. He was taken to a room with a television. The guard said he would like this. In front of him was a football match: Scotland v France. When Scotland scored, Alan jumped up with delight, and nervously looked at the gunman, who smiled. It didn't matter that the recorded game had been played many months earlier.

It was a magical, surreal moment. A moment which showed that the milk of human kindness is within us all and sometimes sport brings it out. Unfortunately Alan never saw the second half as another guard came in and took him away again.

Alan Johnson was finally released on 4 July, after four terrifying months of captivity, but he'll always remember, fondly, that moment of sporting kindness.

"A moment which showed that the milk of human kindness is within us all and sometimes sport brings it out."

2007

Hearts fans honour opposition as Motherwell mourn Phil O'Donnell

Scottish football was in a state of shock and mourning when the captain of Scottish premiere football team Motherwell FC, Phil O'Donnell, collapsed on the pitch whilst playing against Dundee United.

Despite being tended to immediately by doctors and being taken away by ambulance, he was pronounced dead soon after 5pm (29 December 2007). Phil O'Donnell's family, friends, fellow players, Motherwell Football Club and the whole of Scottish football bereaved the loss of this fine footballer.

He played for Motherwell from 1990-'94, Celtic '94-'99, Sheffield Wednesday '99-'03 and once again rejoined Motherwell 04-07. He scored a diving header in the 1991 Scottish Cup Final win against Dundee United (and medals with Celtic in '95 and '98). He also won Scottish PFA Young Player Of The Year award twice (in '92 and '94).

Years later, as a 35 year-old, he played along-side his nephew, David Clarkson (who scored two goals in Phil's final game). He also played for Scotland.

Phil O'Donnell was buried by his beloved wife and their four young children. The funeral was

Motherwell fans pay tribute to Phil O'Donnell
Photograph PA Photos

attended by all of his Motherwell team, the
Dundee United team and fellow footballers from
Celtic, Rangers and football clubs far and wide.

181

A small boy who placed his football shirt along-side the many thousands of shirts,and flowers, had written on his shirt 'God must have needed a captain'.

Although Motherwell's next game after the funeral was cancelled, they eventually had to play again. Their first game after the tragedy was against Hearts Midlothian. When the Motherwell team bus arrived at Hearts FC, the Motherwell team was given a standing ovation by the Hearts fans as they got off the team bus. Phil's requiem mass pamphlet said: 'Divided by team, united in grief.'

"Divided by team, united in grief"

2007

A Stranger lends Mr. Lucey his car to see All Ireland Hurling Final

Stephen Lucey was playing for Limerick in an All Ireland hurling final in Croke Park, Dublin in front of 82,000 fans. Hurling is one of Ireland's two sporting crown jewels that the rest of the world has never discovered. It's an ancient, amateur game and a deep part of Irish culture. It is the fastest field game in the world. The other sport is Gaelic Football (a fast and furious version of rugby and football mixed together).

Hurling requires hugely skillful, savagely fit and totally brave players, not to mention commitment, technique and tactics. Hurling regularly attracts bigger crowds than the English premiership professional matches.

The best of all the 32 counties in Ireland compete against each other. By the time the semi finals come around the country is seething with interest and intrigue. By the time the final comes around, tickets are gold dust. Packed crowds travel to see one of the world's most intense sports on one of the world's finest stages, Dublin's Croke Park.

Limerick had not won an All Ireland Hurling final since 1973. And they had suffered since: losing the 1974, 1981, 1994 and 1996 finals (as well as a semi final in 1980). Their hunger to win an All

Ireland Final was great. The feeling was good. The whole county was on the move. In 2007 Limerick's chance came when they met the mighty Kilkenny in the All Ireland Hurling Final in Croke Park.

As Stephen Lucey's father drove from Limerick to Dublin to see his son play on this historic day, his car suddenly broke down. He was somewhere between Limerick and Dublin; in fact he was in Borrisokane, County Tipperary. He knocked on a door and asked for help in getting the car started again. The owner obliged and came out and tried to start the car but couldn't. When he asked Mr. Lucey where he was going, he discovered that Mr. Lucey was going to Dublin to see the All Ireland Hurling Final with his son playing full back for Limerick. On hearing this, the stranger gave Mr. Lucey the keys of his own car and told him to take it, drive to see his son play and return the car as soon as he could.

Limerick were beaten by Kilkenny and Limerick's moment was gone (at least for that year) but the sporting moment of kindness lives on in the memory of Mr. Lucey Senior and Mr. Lucey Junior.

"the stranger gave Mr. Lucey the keys of his own car and told him to take it, drive to see his son play and return the car as soon as he could"

Limerick's Stephen Lucey (in front) in the heat of battle
with Kilkenny's captain Henry Shefflin in the 2007
All Ireland Hurling Final in Croke Park
Photograph InPhoto

2008

QPR fans acknowledge their nemesis, Andy Cole

Despite scoring a hat trick against QPR, Burnley's
Andy Cole was applauded by the QPR fans
Photograph PA Photos

Queens Park Rangers dreams of reaching the
play-offs in England's championship league (one
below the Premiership) took a drubbing when
they were beaten 4-2 at home to Burnley, having
been 2-0 up.

Burnley striker Andy Cole was having something of a 'dialogue' with the QPR fans as the fans chanted 'you're not famous anymore' (he was once Manchester United and Newcastle's top scorer).

When he scored a goal he rushed up to the QPR fans and gave the 'silence' gesture holding his forefinger to his lips. He scored a second and turned to the QPR fans and slapped his bottom. By the end of the game he had scored a third goal (his first hat trick since playing in a European match for Manchester United, many years previously).

Despite his almost single handed destruction of the QPR fans' dream, the Burnley striker was applauded off the pitch by the QPR home fans in acknowledgement of a masterful performance.

"Despite his almost single handed destruction of the QPR fans' dream, the Burnley striker was applauded off the pitch by the QPR home fans"

2008

American softball teammates carry opponent around the base

Sara Tucholsky, Western Oregon University's softball outfielder, hit the ball over the fence for her first ever home run during her college career. Having hit the ball beautifully, all she had to do was jog around the bases to score a run in this competitive Inter-University, conference game. But her golden moments were short-lived. As she ran past first base, she realised she had rounded the base but hadn't actually touched the bag so she quickly turned and ran back towards it and, in the process, tore her knee ligaments. She collapsed in pain. Effectively, her first home run would not be counted if she didn't run around the base path to complete the home run.

Opposition player, Mallory Holtman, Central Washington University's, first baseman, heard the umpires say that if any of her team mates or coaches helped her, or even touched her, she would be out and no home run scored. So Mallory asked the umpire if she and her team mate Liz Wallace could carry Tucholsky around the bases as she knew the defensive team could carry an opposition player around the bases. Out of courtesy she also asked the opposition coaches if this was ok. They were given permission to do so.

Two of the opposition locked arms and carried

Tucholsky around the pitch stopping at each bag and lowering her foot onto each bag carefully. This home run won the game for her team and eliminated Central Washington from the play-offs.

Central Washington's Liz Wallace, left, and Mallory Holtman help Western Oregon's Sara Tucholsky to score her first ever home run
Photograph PA Photos

When Holtman was asked how she felt she said "It's not like she hit a double or a triple and we were trying to help her. She hit it over the fence. Anyone is deserving of a home run when they hit it over the fence." Liz Wallace's answer to the same question was "It's touched a lot of people and it's a blessing to be a part of that."

Sarah Tucholsky's final comment when interviewed: "I just hope people take out of this story, you know, that instead of worrying about winning and losing, we can worry about in a situation like this, doing something good for people."

"...instead of worrying about winning and losing, we can worry about in a situation like this, doing something good for people."

2008

Opponents and friends 30 years on Higgies Heroes

Great battles are relished amongst great sportsmen and women. The relishing lingers forever. Win or lose, the competitive intensity from great sporting occasions is relived and remembered forever. It just never goes away. Team mates and opposition have a special bonding, a unique respect even when a burning competitive edge remains. That's what makes reunions so special.

When former Cambridge University team mates heard that Alastair Hignell (who played cricket and rugby for Cambridge and England) had Multiple Sclerosis, they decided to help him and other MS sufferers by running in the London Marathon (and raising funds) under the name of 'Higgies Heroes'.

Higgie made his full back debut for England in 1975 (as 19 year old in the brutal 'Battle of Ballymore' in Brisbane Australia) and played 14 times for England, winning his last cap in 1979. He also won his colours at Cambridge in both cricket and rugby union.

After teaching he moved into journalism and worked for BBC Radio. He was diagnosed with Multiple Sclerosis in 2000 and was forced to retire due to his condition in 2008. He kept it private until an old friend repeatedly asked him about his limp. When he reluctantly revealed his condition, his former team mates rallied around as in days gone by. They formed a group called 'Higgies Heroes' and raised money by running in marathons.

Alastair says: "It always stuns me when people rally round like this. My mates in rugby and journalism came good for me. The number of good people out there is amazing, so caring and generous. It is life-affirming to find that people are so good.

Alastair Hignell playing for England
Photograph PA Photos

"It always stuns me .... The number of good people out there is amazing, so caring and generous."

2008

Opponents and friends 60 years on Ireland and Wales

As mentioned in Higgies Heroes, great battles are relished amongst great sportsmen and women. Team-mates and opposition have a special bonding, a unique respect, a particular private club where opponents become friends for life.

2008 saw the 60 year celebration of Ireland's only grand slam winning team, the 1948 side that beat everyone. A photograph used on the Irish Rugby Football Union's web site shows six Irish players from that team, along with two of their opposing Welsh players from that final game against Wales in Belfast.

The Men of '48 Jimmy Nelson, Bertie O'Hanlon, Jack Kyle, Michael O'Flanagan, Paddy Reid, Jim McCarthy with former Welsh players Bleddyn Williams & Jack Matthews (front right). Der Healy and John Lyons, IRFU (back row L&R)

Photograph Sports File

Rugby's unique code of honour extends beyond shaking hands with the opposition and even applauding the opposition off the pitch. It can extend right through to inviting the opposition into your team photos 60 years after the final whistle.

"Team mates and opposition have a special bonding, a unique respect, a unique private club where opponents become friends for life."

2008

Opponents and Friends 70 years on – the Australian Invincibles & England

At the time when the world witnessed the greatest batsman ever seen, Australia's Sir Donald Bradman, there was one man who could somehow bowl him out. England's Sir Alec Bedser is the last living man to dismiss the world's greatest cricketer, Sir Don Bradman, in a Test match.

Alec Bedser hunted Sir Donald and bowled him out on several occasions. Bedser, however, confirms that Bradman was indeed the finest batsman ever. He once hit 300 runs in just one day in the Leeds Test of 1930. His world record test batting average still stands today. In fact that Australian team was packed with stars. They were so good they became known worldwide as 'The Invincibles'.

Bedser, today, is 90 years old and remembers his England debut a home test against India in which he took 11 wickets in a remarkable debut. He was an extremely accurate medium-fast seam bowler. He went on to become the first Englishman to take 200 Test wickets. However it was 'The Invincibles' who left an indelible impression on Bedser. In fact many of them became good friends.

"I was friendly with them all," says Bedser in a

BBC interview. "We were friends. I don't see no reason not to be. I found them all a good lot of blokes."

Although Sir Donald was a very private man, he and Sir Alec became close friends and exchanged intimate letters particularly when Sir Donald's beautiful wife, Jessie, was dying of cancer (she passed away in 1997 and Sir Donald passed away in 2001). Bedser was delighted to see two of the Invincibles step off a plane 70 years later to celebrate Bedser's 90th birthday. Australia's Arthur Morris and Neil Harvey made the long trip to help Bedser celebrate his 90th birthday. Age old adversaries yet friends for life.

Don Bradman is out caught by Len Hutton (not pictured) bowled by Alec Bedser, England v Australia Test, Lords
Photograph PA Photos

"Age old adversaries yet friends for life."

See 1948 A Sad Celebration, A Standing Ovation and 3 Cheers from the Opposition for more on Sir Donald.

2008

101 year old Marathon Runner Buster Martin helps next generation

Buster Martin is 101 years old and ran the London Marathon to raise money for the Rhys Daniels Trust, which helps parents of children who have life threatening illnesses by providing a 'home from home' so they can stay with their children. "There's nothing worse than a child in a bad way and its parents can't afford to stay there with them" says Buster who already held world titles for the oldest person to run 5K, 10k and half marathon (5 hours & 13 minutes). He completed the 2008 marathon a little over 10 hours (the exact time is not known since the time keepers had packed up and gone home.

After more than 5 hours and finishing the half marathon, Buster's first words were: "Where's my beer?" He still made it into work on time on Monday morning, where the MD, Charlie Mullins said he was "amazed and delighted; he turned up on time and set to work polishing the vans. He's a revelation."

When not working three days a week, Buster spends time in a nearby boxing gym working with a pair of trainers who help him prepare for his next race. Charly Mullins says Buster is a "great inspiration, he's got a million stories to tell, he is so knowledgeable." Mens magazine, FHM, signed him up as an agony uncle giving help and advice to a younger generation. The ex-member of rock band, The Zimmers, Buster has 17 children. The Zimmers with a combined age of over 3,000 years, had a hit single in 2007 with a cover of The Who's 'My Generation'. Busters advice to aspiring runners or rock stars is to "not think about it too much. Just do it."

Buster Martin: "I may not be a millionaire in money but I'm a millionaire in health"
Photograph PA Photos

When asked 'what kind of time do you hope for?' Buster answered "In time for the first pint of beer." Will he run again? "In 50 years, when I'm 150 years old." Although there is some debate about Buster's exact age, he did finish the marathon in a little over ten hours. His exact time will not be known until a later date because the tracking system which records the runners' times was removed at 7pm (almost an hour before Buster crossed the finishing line). "I may not be a millionaire in money but I'm a millionaire in health"

"I may not be a millionaire in money but I'm a millionaire in health"

2008

He Junquan, the Quintessential Sportsman, Beijing

He Junquan is an extraordinary athlete. Having lost both of his arms in a frightening electrical accident when he was three years old, he decided that he would develop some new skills and become a world class swimmer.

He won a gold, a silver and a bronze medal for China in the Sydney 2000 Paralympics. He then went on to win four golds in Athens 2004. When he arrived in Beijing 2008, many people were just getting to know him. Those that did know him, felt that even without arms he could win gold. He has a focused look of steely determination in his eyes as he waits for the starter gun.

The favourite, He Junquan leaps for glory in the SM5 Final of the men's 200m indvidual medley
Photograph Photoshot

He Junquan reguarly beats other swimmers (who have arms) and was fancied as favourite for the men's 200m individual medley.

When he hit the water in Beijing's Water Cube, he swam brilliantly, passing many other swimmers who had arms.

His only way of stopping is by smacking his head against the tiles at the end of the pool. He often leaves the pool with a headache or a neck or back injury. He must have done this thousands of times during the intense training that swimmers go through.

As he came to the finish and prepared to crash head first into the tiles again, he slowed down slightly to lessen the impact. Brazilian Daniel Dias touched the wall first with an outstretched hand. He Junquan was beaten.

Despite being pipped at the post, he revels in the cut and thrust of top level competition. Despite being beaten, Junquan is a real winner, his smile says it all (see next page) as he congratulated Brazil's Dias who took the gold at the SM5 final of men's 200m individual medley. Junquan took silver.

Despite being beaten, the quintessential sportsman Hu Junquan's smile says it all.
Photograph Photoshot

"Despite being beaten, Junquan is a real winner, a true sportsman. His smile says it all"

Conclusion
& Invitation to visit
the
Great Moments of Sportsmanship Club

We are all capable of great deeds – whether in front of 1 billion viewers or on a wet grey afternoon with one man and his dog watching a non league game unfold. Those moments of the extended hand shake, the embrace and the welcome pint of beer after the contest can mean as much as the game itself.

The generosity of the human spirit, knows no bounds. It lies dormant until tapped. But we live in an age where gamesmanship, sledging, diving, booing, spitting and psyching out the opposition have become the accepted norm. You can help to redress the balance by telling us your own stories of great moments of sportsmanship which you have experienced or heard about. Post them to me Paul Smith at

www.GreatMomentsOfSportsmanship.com

Ask other people for their stories. Post them too. Let's get these stories into the minds and hearts of young players and coaches coming through the ranks. Let's get coaches, teachers, commentators and opinion formers exchanging stories and encouraging sports people to be great sportsmen and women.

Lastly, if you have any comments, corrections, amendments, additions or challenges about any of the stories – please post them to me at www.TheGreatMomentsOfSportsmanship.com Go online to the Great Moments Of Sportsmanship Club - a web site where you tell your story, read others, add comments, discuss each others (and vote for your favourites) as well as watching many of these great moments in action.

www.GreatMomentsOfSportsmanship.com

About the Author

Dubliner PR Smith lives in London. He played rugby and football in St. Michael's College, Dublin, Hurling in Collaiste na Rinne, Waterford, rugby, golf, tennis, gaelic football, football, table tennis, basketball and snooker in Rockwell College. He won a Gleeson Cup medal (All Ireland Vocational Colleges Rugby) playing for the College of Commerce. Two years later Paul captained the team to win a second Gleeson Cup.

He then played for Lansdowne RFC before moving to London Irish RFC where he played for the Nomads for twenty years. He also coached junior rugby for eight years.

Paul has written four other books on marketing (including his SOSTAC ® Planning Model). His books are translated into seven languages.
See www.PRSmith.org

A percentage of all profits from this book is donated to three charities: The Stuart Mangan Appeal, Right To Play and Clic Sargent - see next page.

www.PRSmith.org

Causes that this book supports

A percentage of all profits from the sale of this book is donated to these three causes:

The Stuart Mangan Appeal
On Saturday April 5th 2008, a simple tackle in a club rugby game in London left Stuart Mangan, a graduate of Rockwell College and UCC aged just 24, with a devastating spinal injury. Stuart is completely paralyzed from the neck down and unable to breathe without a ventilator. Stuart will require 24-hour medical care for the rest of his life. www.StuartMangan.org

Right To Play
Right To Play is an humanitarian organization that uses sport and play programs to improve health, develop life skills, and foster peace for children and communities in disadvantaged areas. They train local community leaders as Coaches 20+ countries affected by war, poverty, and disease in Africa, Asia and the Middle East. www.RightToPlay.com

Clic Sargent
Clic Sargent Care for children and young people with cancer and their families in hospital and the community. When a child is diagnosed with cancer it can seem like normal life stops and a different journey begins. It's a journey that tests families physically, emotionally, socially and financially. www.clicsargent.org